S. Hrg. 114–77

# U.S. POLICY IN UKRAINE: COUNTERING RUSSIA AND DRIVING REFORM

## HEARING

BEFORE THE

## COMMITTEE ON FOREIGN RELATIONS UNITED STATES SENATE

ONE HUNDRED FOURTEENTH CONGRESS

FIRST SESSION

MARCH 10, 2015

Printed for the use of the Committee on Foreign Relations

Available via the World Wide Web: http://www.gpo.gov/fdsys/

U.S. GOVERNMENT PUBLISHING OFFICE

96–831 PDF          WASHINGTON : 2015

For sale by the Superintendent of Documents, U.S. Government Publishing Office
Internet: bookstore.gpo.gov   Phone: toll free (866) 512–1800; DC area (202) 512–1800
Fax: (202) 512–2104   Mail: Stop IDCC, Washington, DC 20402–0001

(II)

# CONTENTS

# U.S. POLICY IN UKRAINE: COUNTERING RUSSIA AND DRIVING REFORM

## TUESDAY, MARCH 10, 2015

U.S. SENATE,
COMMITTEE ON FOREIGN RELATIONS,
*Washington, DC.*

The committee met, pursuant to notice, at 10:03 a.m., in room SD–419, Dirksen Senate Office Building, Hon. Bob Corker (chairman of the committee) presiding.

Present: Senators Corker, Risch, Rubio, Johnson, Flake, Gardner, Perdue, Isakson, Paul, Barrasso, Menendez, Cardin, Shaheen, Murphy, and Kaine.

### OPENING STATEMENT OF HON. BOB CORKER, U.S. SENATOR FROM TENNESSEE

The CHAIRMAN. This meeting of the Senate Foreign Relations Committee will come to order.

I want to begin this hearing by expressing my condolences to the family of Boris Nemtsov and the people of Russia. The murder of Russian opposition leader, Boris Nemtsov, just outside the Kremlin appears to be an attempt to silence those in Russia who want to see their country move away from the authoritarianism, corruption, and lawlessness of today's Russia. Boris Nemtsov sought a better future for his people, and we must remain committed to his vision for a democratic Russia at peace with itself and its neighbors. He was especially critical of Putin's aggression in Ukraine where, for over a year now, Russia has continued its occupation of Crimea and the destabilization of the country's eastern regions.

Our country made a commitment in 1994 to defend Ukraine's sovereignty and its territorial integrity, which has been under a near constant assault by Russia for more than a year. More recently, we lured Ukraine West by supporting their desire for closer association with Europe.

Now with Ukraine's future in the balance, the refusal of the administration to step up with more robust support for Ukraine and further pressure on Russia is a blight on U.S. policy and 70 years of defending a Europe that is whole, democratic, and free.

The conflict in eastern Ukraine, started by Russian-backed mercenaries, now directly involves thousands of Russian military personnel and has resulted in over 6,000 deaths and generated 1.5 million refugees and internally displaced persons.

For roughly 2 weeks after the second Minsk cease-fire agreement was signed on February 12, the Russian-backed rebels continued their offensive activities, ultimately acquiring the strategic railway hub, Debaltseve. The determination of the rebels to secure Debaltseve, despite the fact that the Minsk cease-fire agreement required them to withdraw to a demarcation line established last September, shows that Putin has no intention of honoring the cease-fire.

While the violence has subsided since the rebels achieved their short-term objective and acquired Debaltseve, the Minsk cease-fire is far from being a success.

In addition to the ambiguous constitutional electoral conditions required of Ukraine to regain control of its borders, the second Minsk agreement is burdened by the failure of the first Minsk agreement as it stands. In fact, administration officials have repeatedly referred to the recent Minsk accord as an implementation agreement of the first Minsk accord.

But jumping from cease-fire to cease-fire in hope of convincing Russian-backed rebels to fulfill the same commitments they continually renege on is not a strategy and certainly not a strategy for success.

In my view, any strategy will not be effective unless the United States begins to provide Ukraine with the ability to inflict serious military cost using defensive weapons on the thousands of Russian troops operating in its eastern regions.

The Ukraine Freedom Support Act, which originated in this committee, passed unanimously by Congress, and signed into law by the President, authorizes $350 million in lethal military assistance to Ukraine. But yesterday we heard Germany's Ambassador to the United States say that President Obama privately pledged to Chancellor Merkel in February that the United States will not deliver lethal military assistance to Ukraine despite the fact that he and other administration officials continue to tell the American public that they are seriously considering this policy.

Deputy Secretary of State Tony Blinken argued last week in Berlin that no amount of lethal military assistance for Ukraine will be sufficient to defeat the rebels and their Russian sponsors.

But our objective is not to provide Ukraine with enough weapons to overwhelm the Russian military in a direct confrontation. Rather, the provision of lethal assistance aims to increase Ukraine's defense capabilities in a way that will give Kyiv the ability to produce conditions on the ground favorable to a genuine peace process.

By equipping Ukraine with the means to impose a greater military cost on Russia, the United States will be contributing to a quicker, fairer, and more stable settlement of the conflict.

But our support for Ukraine must go beyond simply imposing cost on Russia. Ukraine's foreign currency reserves have diminished to a month's worth of imports. The Ukrainian currency has lost 80 percent of its value since April 2014, and its economy continues to teeter on the brink of collapse.

At the same time, while I believe the government in Kyiv is genuinely committed to reform, more needs to be done by the Ukrainian authorities to move forward with these reforms, especially in the energy sector where corruption siphons billions of dollars away from the budget each year.

Even if the United States does more to help Ukraine and Kyiv defeats the Russian-backed rebels, but the Ukrainian economy implodes in the process, we have failed and Putin has succeeded. As a matter of fact, he has had an even greater success if that occurs.

This is why the United States must have a comprehensive strategy that will both counter Russian aggression but also drive political, economic, and anticorruption reforms in Ukraine.

During this hearing, I hope to have a detailed discussion that explores the situation in eastern Ukraine since the Minsk cease-fire agreement was signed, examines why the United States has failed to provide Ukraine with lethal military assistance, and considers additional ways to support Ukraine with its ongoing economic challenges.

I look forward to your testimony. I thank you for being here.

And now I will turn it over to our distinguished ranking member for his opening comments.

### STATEMENT OF HON. ROBERT MENENDEZ, U.S. SENATOR FROM NEW JERSEY

Senator MENENDEZ. Well, thank you, Mr. Chairman, for holding what is an extraordinarily important and timely hearing on countering Russia in the Ukraine. And I appreciate our witnesses being here.

Let me join you in very heartfelt condolences to someone who was a courageous opposition leader, and sometimes true patriots pay a price. Boris Nemtsov led efforts in which he passionately believed in in a different Russia. And I find it pretty outrageous to see the latest narrative that is being portrayed that an Islamist plot is the reason why he was assassinated. But to his family, his friends, and his followers, we have our heartfelt thoughts and condolences.

Now, as it relates to today's hearing, there are many experts who would contend that the complexity of the geopolitics that led to the U.S. retreat from Europe created an opening for Putin in the Ukraine. Clearly, we must closely coordinate with our European friends for the sanctions against Russia to work.

But I think, without any doubt, we can all agree on one point, and that is that the United States must take the lead. I believe the administration should fully implement measures in the Ukraine Freedom Support Act, which the President signed into law on December 18. The legislation passed with unanimous consent in both Houses of Congress. It authorizes the President to provide much-needed military and humanitarian aid to Ukraine, and it imposes additional sanctions against Russia. This legislation was necessary in December, and it is certainly necessary today.

Now, we all want a diplomatic solution, but I believe this can only come about when Putin believes that the cost of continuing to ravage Ukraine is simply too high. Providing nonlethal equipment like night vision goggles is all well and good, but giving the Ukrainians the ability to see Russians coming but not the weapons to stop them is not the answer. The night vision goggles are one thing, but providing antitank and antiarmor weapons, tactical troop-operated surveillance drones, secure command and communications equipment would be far better.

And frankly, I am disappointed that the administration, required to report to Congress on its plan for increasing military assistance to Ukraine on February 15, has yet to send us that report. I was glad to join with Senator Corker in sending a letter to the President yesterday on the importance of providing defensive weapons and that we need to see this overdue report.

In my view, it is time to impose additional targeted sanctions on the Russian energy sector to add to existing sanctions that are already costing the Russian economy about $140 billion per year, or about 7 percent of its economy. The administration should tighten restrictions on the development of shale deposits or to drilling and offshore drilling. I think the last thing we want to do is use American technology to create a Russian shale revolution that could only extend its reach into Europe and beyond.

The Ukraine Freedom Support Act called for the administration to impose sanctions on other defense industry targets as well as on special Russian crude oil projects by January 31, and I am still waiting for the administration's response.

At the end of the day, the most effective sanction is an economically viable and stable Ukraine. The United States may provide an additional $1 billion in loan guarantees toward the end of this year, on top of the $2 billion in guarantees already provided. In my view, this is a worthy investment, and it needs to be matched by continued reforms by the Ukrainians.

Finally, I think we need to reinforce the transatlantic agenda. We must take a more strategic approach in facing this resurgent Russia. First, we need to reinvigorate the institutions that have for so long contributed to the transatlantic relationship and peace and stability. We need to sharpen our arsenal of response options, and that means NATO and EU integration and adapting them to today's realities.

In my view, the attention on Europe's east in confronting the threat from Russia has been necessary, but we also need to focus on the south, also vulnerable to undue Russian influence. We need to strengthen secure and economic relationships in the Balkans, especially in Serbia, Montenegro, Bulgaria, and Bosnia.

Second, our intelligence community also needs to reprioritize the Russian threat not only by addressing the immediate security threat in Ukraine, but across the board in Europe.

And third is communications. I understand the administration is working with the Broadcasting Board of Governors to commit a little over $23 million to Russian language programming, which is a 49-percent increase over fiscal year 2014. I think that and other public diplomacy funds are incredibly important to counter Russian propaganda which, when I traveled to the region last year and have listened to those who have visited us from the region, they said they are overwhelmed by Russian propaganda.

There is one key point, and at the end of the day, that is that strong American leadership is what will matter.

Mr. Chairman, I would ask that the totality of my statement be included in the record, and I thank you for the opportunity.

[The prepared statement of Senator Menendez follows:]

## Prepared Statement of Senator Robert Menendez

### American Leadership

There are many experts who would contend that the complexity of the geopolitics that led to the U.S.'s retreat from Europe created an opening for Putin in Ukraine . . . . Clearly, we must work in close coordination with our European friends in order for the sanctions against Russia to work. . . . But, I think—without any doubt— we can all agree on one key point: The United States must take the lead.

The administration should fully implement measures in the Ukraine Freedom Support Act, which the President signed into law on December 18. The legislation passed—with unanimous consent—in both Houses of Congress. It authorizes the President to provide much-needed military and humanitarian aid to Ukraine. And it imposes additional sanctions against Russia. This legislation was necessary in December, and is even more necessary today.

### Security Assistance in Ukraine

The simple fact is—we all want a diplomatic solution, but I believe that this can only come about when Putin believes that the cost of continuing to ravage Ukraine is simply too high. We have a responsibility to increase that cost.

Providing nonlethal equipment like night vision goggles is all-well-and-good, but giving Ukrainians the ability to see the Russians coming, but not the weapons to respond, is not the answer. Night vision goggles are one thing, but providing anti-tank and antiarmor weapons, tactical troop-operated surveillance drones, and secure command-and-communications equipment would be better. Frankly, I'm disappointed that the administration—required to report to Congress on its plan for increasing military assistance to Ukraine on February 15—has yet to send us that report.

### Sanctions

In the meantime, Putin has used his military power to impose his will in Ukraine, but he is also using every economic tool at his disposal and we must do the same.

In my view, it's time to impose additional targeted sanctions on the Russian energy sector to add to existing sanctions that are already costing the Russian economy about $140 billion per year—or about 7 percent of its economy. The administration should tighten restrictions on the development of shale deposits, Arctic drilling, and offshore drilling.

The Ukraine Freedom Support Act called for the administration to impose sanctions on other defense industry targets as well as on special Russian crude oil projects by January 31. And I am still waiting on the administration's response. These sanctions are necessary, but, at the end of the day, the most effective sanction is an economically viable and stable Ukraine. The U.S. may provide an additional $1 billion in loan guarantees toward the end of this year, on top of the $2 billion in guarantees already provided. In my view, this is a worthy investment and it needs to be matched by continued reforms by the Ukrainians.

As I said—all of us can agree on one key point: at the end of the day, strong American leadership is what will matter most.

With that, I thank the Chairman for calling this hearing, and I thank our witnesses for taking time to be here.

The CHAIRMAN. Without objection, absolutely. We want to thank you for the comments.

And we will turn to the witnesses. On our first panel, our first witness is Victoria Nuland, Assistant Secretary of State for European and Eurasian Affairs. Our second witness today is Brian McKeon, Principal Deputy Under Secretary of Defense for Policy. A big title. Thank you. Our third witness is Ramin Toloui, Assistant Secretary of Treasury for International Finance. Our fourth and final witness on the first panel is Vice Adm. Frank Pandolfe, Director for Strategic Plans and Policy at the Joint Staff. We thank you all for being here, sharing your thoughts and viewpoints.

I will remind you that your full statement will be entered into the record, without objection. And so if you would please summarize your statement, about 5 minutes or so, and we look forward to our questions. Again, thank you all very much for being here.

## STATEMENT OF HON. VICTORIA NULAND, ASSISTANT SECRETARY OF STATE FOR EUROPEAN AND EURASIAN AFFAIRS, U.S. DEPARTMENT OF STATE, WASHINGTON, DC

Ms. NULAND. Thank you, Chairman Corker, Ranking Member Menendez, members of this committee. Thank you for the opportunity to join you today to talk about the situation in Ukraine and for the personal investment that so many of you have made in that country's future.

Today Ukraine is central to our 25-year transatlantic quest for a Europe whole, free, and at peace. My interagency colleagues and I are pleased to update you on United States efforts to support Ukraine as it works to liberate the country from its corrupt, oligarchic past, and chart a more democratic European future and to bring an end to the Russian and separatist aggression.

In my remarks, I will focus on two areas today: first, the work that Ukraine is doing with U.S. and international support to reform the country, to tackle corruption, and to strengthen democratic institutions. Second, I will give an update on our efforts to support the implementation of the February and September Minsk agreements, including our readiness to impose further costs on Russia if the commitments Moscow made are further violated.

Ukraine's leaders in the executive branch and the Parliament know that they are in a race against time and external pressure to clean up the country and enact the difficult and socially painful reforms required to kick-start the economy and to meet their commitments to their own people, to the IMF, and to international community.

The package of reforms already put forward by the government and enacted by the Rada is impressive in its scope and in its political courage. Just last week, the Ukrainians passed budget reform, which is expected to slash the deficit significantly this year and to give more fiscal control to local communities and spur economic and political decentralization.

They have made tough choices in just the last few days to reduce and cap pension benefits and to phase in a higher retirement age, as requested by the IMF.

They have created new banking provisions to stiffen penalties for stripping assets from the banks at the public's expense, a common practice among oligarchs.

And they have passed laws cutting wasteful gas subsidies and closing the space for corrupt middlemen who buy low, sell high, and rip off the Ukrainian people.

Ukraine will use the $400 million in increased revenue from these measures to care for the 1.7 million people who have been driven from their homes by the conflict.

With United States support, with your support on this committee, and in this Congress, including a $1 billion loan guarantee last year and $355 million in foreign assistance and technical advisors, the Ukrainian Government is improving energy efficiency in homes and factories with metering, consumer incentives, and infrastructure improvements, building e-governance platforms to make procurement more transparent and basic government services cleaner and more publicly accessible.

They are putting a newly trained force of beat cops on the streets in Kyiv who will protect not shake down the citizens, a prototype of what they hope to do nationwide.

They are reforming the Prosecutor General's Office, supported by U.S. law enforcement and criminal justice advisors to help energize law enforcement and increase prosecutions.

With the help of USAID experts, they are deregulating the agriculture sector and allowing family farmers to sell more of their produce in local and regional and wholesale markets.

And they are helping those who were forced to flee Donetsk and Luhansk with new jobs and skills training in places like Kharkiv.

And there is more support on the way. The President's fiscal year 2016 budget request includes $513.5 million to build on these efforts.

And as you said, Mr. Ranking Member and Mr. Chairman, Ukraine's hard work must continue. Between now and the summer, we must see continued budget discipline and tax collection enforced across the country, notably including on some of Ukraine's richest citizens who have enjoyed tax impunity for far too long. We need to see continued reforms at Naftogaz and across the energy sector. We need to see final passage of agricultural legislation, full and impartial implementation of anticorruption measures, including a commitment to break the oligarchic, kleptocratic culture that has ripped off the country for too long.

As you both said in your opening statements, the best antidote to Russian aggression and malign influence is for Ukraine to succeed as a democratic, free market state. For this to happen, we have to help ensure that the Ukrainian Government lives up to its promises to its own people and keeps the trust of the international financial community. But at the same time, the United States and Europe and the international community must keep faith with Ukraine and help ensure that Russia's aggression and meddling cannot crash Ukraine's spirit, its will, or its economy before reforms take hold.

That brings me to my second point. Even as Ukraine is building a more peaceful, democratic, independent nation across 93 percent of its territory, Crimea and parts of eastern Ukraine have suffered a reign of terror. In eastern Ukraine, Russia and its separatist puppets have unleashed unspeakable violence and pillage. This is a manufactured conflict, controlled by the Kremlin, fueled by Russian tanks and heavy weapons, and financed at Russian taxpayers' expense. It has cost the lives of more than 6,000 Ukrainians, and hundreds of young Russians have also lost their lives in eastern Ukraine, sent there to fight and die by the Kremlin. And when they come home in zinc coffins, ''Cargo 200'' which is the Russian euphemism for war dead, their mothers and their wives and their children are told not to ask too many questions or raise a fuss if they ever want to see death benefits.

Throughout this conflict, the United States and the EU have worked in lockstep to impose successive rounds of tough sanctions, including sectoral sanctions, on Russia and its separatist cronies as the cost for their actions. Our unity with Europe remains the cornerstone of our policy toward this crisis and a fundamental source of our strength.

It is in that spirit that we salute the efforts of German Chancellor Merkel and French President Hollande in Minsk on February 12 to try again to end the fighting in eastern Ukraine. The Minsk package of agreements, the September 5th and 19th agreements and the February 12th implementing agreement, offer a real opportunity for peace, disarmament, political normalization and decentralization in Ukraine, and the return of Ukrainian state sovereignty in the east and border control.

For some eastern Ukrainians, conditions have already begun to improve. The OSCE reports that the cease-fire is holding on many parts of the line of contact. There have been significant withdrawals already of Government of Ukraine heavy weapons, and some separatist heavy weapons have also been withdrawn, although that process is incomplete, as is OSCE access. And the little village in southeast Donetsk of Komintermove demining has already begun under OSCE auspices.

But the picture is very mixed. Just yesterday, shelling continued in Shyrokyne, a key village on the way to Mariupol, and outside Donetsk over the weekend. As I said, access for OSCE monitors, particularly in separatist-controlled areas, remains spotty. And just in the last few days, we can confirm new transfers of Russian tanks, armored vehicles, heavy artillery, and rocket equipment over the border to the separatists in eastern Ukraine.

So in the coming days—days, not weeks—here is what we need to see: a complete cease-fire in all parts of eastern Ukraine; full, unfettered access to the whole conflict zone; a pull-back of all heavy weapons; and an end to uninspected convoys of cargo over the Ukrainian border.

If fully implemented, this will bring greater peace and security in eastern Ukraine for the first time in almost a year.

As the President has said, we will judge Russia by its actions not by its words. And the United States will, with our international partners, start rolling back sanctions on Russia but only when the Minsk agreements are fully implemented.

The reverse is also true. If these are not implemented, there will be more sanctions, and we have already begun consultations with our European partners on further sanctions pressure, should Russia continue fueling the fire in the east or in other parts of Ukraine, fail to implement Minsk, or grab more land, as we saw in Debaltseve after the agreements were signed.

Mr. Chairman, Mr. Ranking Member, members of this committee, America's investment in Ukraine is about far more than protecting the choice of a single European country. It is about protecting the rules-based system across Europe and globally. It is about saying no to borders changed by force, to big countries intimidating their neighbors or demanding a sphere of influence.

We thank this committee for its bipartisan support and commitment to the sovereignty and territorial integrity of Ukraine and to a Europe whole, free, and at peace. Thank you.

[The prepared statement of Ms. Nuland follows:]

PREPARED STATEMENT OF VICTORIA NULAND

Chairman Corker, Ranking Member Menendez and members of this committee—thank you for the opportunity to speak to you today on the situation in Ukraine and for your personal investment in that country's future. As many of you know from your travels, your meetings, and the establishment of the bipartisan Senate Ukraine Caucus last month, Ukrainians deeply appreciate this committee's support for their country's security, democracy, sovereignty, and future prosperity.

Today Ukraine is central to our 25-year Transatlantic quest for a ''Europe whole, free, and at peace.'' My interagency colleagues and I are pleased to update you today on U.S. efforts to support Ukraine as it works to liberate the country from its corrupt, oligarchic past, chart a more democratic, European future, and bring an end to Russian-fueled violence. In my remarks, I'll focus on two areas: first, the work Ukraine is doing—with U.S. and international support—to reform the country, tackle corruption, and strengthen democratic institutions; second, I will give an update on our efforts to support implementation of the February and September Minsk Agreements, including our readiness to impose further costs on Russia if the commitments Moscow made are further violated. My colleagues from DOD—Principal Deputy Under Secretary McKeon and Vice Admiral Pandolfe—will address our security relationship in greater detail. A/S Toloui will speak more to our macroeconomic assistance in coordination with our international partners.

First—a quick reminder of why we're here. Sixteen months ago, the Kyiv Maidan and towns across Ukraine erupted in peaceful protest by ordinary Ukrainians fed up with a sleazy, corrupt regime bent on cheating the people of their sovereign choice to associate with Europe. They braved frigid temperatures, brutal beatings, and sniper bullets. The leader of that rotten regime fled the country, and he was voted out by the Parliament—including most members of his own party. Then, Ukraine began to forge a new nation on its own terms—signing an Association Agreement with the European Union; holding free and fair elections—twice—even as fighting raged in the east; and undertaking deep and comprehensive economic and political reforms.

Against the backdrop of Russia's aggression, the situation in the country remains precarious. Ukraine's leaders, in the executive branch and the Parliament, know they are in a race against time to clean up the country and enact the difficult and socially painful reforms required to kick start the economy, and meet their commitments to their people, the IMF and the international community. The package of reforms already put forward by the government, and enacted by the Rada, is impressive in its scope and political courage.

Just last week:

- They passed budget reform expected to slash the deficit this year, and strengthen decentralization by giving more fiscal control to local communities;
- They made tough choices to reduce and cap pension benefits, increase work requirements, and phase in a higher retirement age;
- They created a new banking provision to stiffen penalties for financiers for stripping assets from banks at the public's expense, a common practice among oligarchs;
- And, they passed laws cutting wasteful gas subsidies and closing the space for corrupt middlemen that buy low, sell high, and rip off the Ukrainian people. These laws will also enhance corporate efficiency, incentivize domestic production, and use $400 million in increased revenue from state-owned gas companies to help care for the poor including some of the 1.7 million people driven from their homes by the conflict.

With U.S. support—including a $1 billion loan guarantee last year and $355 million in foreign assistance and technical advisors—the Ukrainian Government is:

- Helping insulate vulnerable Ukrainians from the impact of necessary economic reforms;
- Improving energy efficiency in homes and factories with metering, consumer incentives, and infrastructure improvement;
- Building e-governance platforms to make procurement transparent and basic government services cleaner and publicly accessible;
- Putting a newly trained force of beat cops on the streets of Kyiv who will protect, not shake down, the citizens;
- Reforming the Prosecutor General's Office (PGO)—supported by U.S. law enforcement and criminal justice advisors—and helping energize law enforcement and just prosecutions;
- Moving to bring economic activity out of the shadows;

- Supporting new agriculture laws—with the help of USAID experts—to deregulate the sector and allow family farms to sell their produce in local, regional and wholesale markets, and;
- Helping those forced to flee Donetsk and Luhansk with USAID jobs and skills training programs in places like Kharkiv.

And there's more support on the way. The President's budget includes an FY16 request of $513.5 million—almost six times more than our FY14 request—to build on these efforts.

To turn the page, Ukraine's hard work must continue. Between now and the summer, we must see budget discipline maintained and tax collection enforced across the country—notably including on some of Ukraine's richest citizens who have enjoyed impunity for too long. We need to see continued reforms at Naftogaz and across the energy sector; final passage of agriculture legislation; full and impartial implementation of anticorruption measures, including a commitment to break the oligarchic, kleptocratic culture have has decimated the country.

As I said in my last appearance before this committee, the most lasting antidote to Russian aggression and malign influence in the medium term is for Ukraine to succeed as a democratic, free market state and to beat back the corruption, dependence, and external pressure that have thwarted Ukrainians' aspirations for decades. For this to happen, we must ensure that the government lives up to its promises to the Ukrainian people, and keeps the trust of the international financial community. And, at the same time, the United States, Europe, and the international community must keep faith with Ukraine, and help insure that Russia's aggression and meddling can't crash Ukraine's spirit, its will, or its economy before reforms take hold.

Which brings me to my second point—even as Ukraine is building a peaceful, democratic, independent nation across 93 percent of its territory, Crimea and parts of eastern Ukraine are suffering a reign of terror. Today Crimea remains under illegal occupation and human rights abuses are the norm, not the exception, for many at-risk groups there—Crimean Tatars, Ukrainians who won't surrender their passports, journalists, LGBT citizens and others.

In eastern Ukraine, Russia and its separatist puppets unleashed unspeakable violence and pillage. This manufactured conflict—controlled by the Kremlin; fueled by Russian tanks and heavy weapons; financed at Russian taxpayers' expense—has cost the lives of more than 6,000 Ukrainians, but also of hundreds of young Russians sent to fight and die there by the Kremlin, in a war their government denies. When they come home in zinc coffins—''Cargo 200,'' the Russian euphemism for war dead—their mothers, wives, and children are told not to ask too many questions or raise a fuss if they want to see any death benefits.

Throughout this conflict, the United States and the EU have worked in lock-step to impose successive rounds of tough sanctions—including sectoral sanctions—on Russia and its separatist cronies as the costs for their actions. In Crimea, we have shown through our investment sanctions that if you bite off a piece of another country, it will dry up in your mouth. Our unity with Europe remains the cornerstone of our policy toward this crisis.

And it is in that spirit that we salute the efforts of German Chancellor Merkel and French President Hollande in Minsk on February 12 to try again to end the fighting in Ukraine's East. The Minsk Package of Agreements—September 5, September 19, and the February 12 implementing agreement—offer a real opportunity for peace, disarmament, political normalization and decentralization in eastern Ukraine, and the return of Ukrainian state sovereignty and control of its territory and borders. Russia agreed to it; Ukraine agreed to it; the separatists agreed to it. And the international community stands behind it.

For some eastern Ukrainians, conditions have begun to improve. Along long areas of the line of contact, particularly in Luhansk Oblast, the cease-fire has taken hold; the guns have quieted in some towns and villages; some weapons have been withdrawn; some hostages have been released.

But the picture is very mixed. Since the February 15 cease-fire, the OSCE Special Monitoring Mission has recorded hundreds of violations. Debaltseve, a key rail hub beyond the cease-fire lines, fell to the separatists and Russian forces 6 days after Minsk was signed and 3 days after the cease-fire was to come into effect. In Shchastya, in villages near the Donetsk Airport, in Shyrokyne and other towns around Mariupol the shelling continues, as verified by OSCE Special Monitor Authority.

In the coming days, not weeks or months—here is what we need to see:

- A complete cease-fire in all parts of eastern Ukraine.

- Full, unfettered access to the whole conflict zone including all separatist-held territory, for OSCE monitors, and;
- A full pull-back of all heavy weapons—Ukrainian, Russian, and separatist—as stipulated in the agreements, under OSCE monitoring and verification.

If fully implemented, this will bring greater peace and security in eastern Ukraine for the first time in almost a year. And with it, Ukraine will once again have unfettered access to its own people in the East, and the opportunity for dialogue and political normalization with them. That's what Minsk promises. Peace, then political normalization, then a return of the border. But first, there must be peace.

Russia's commitments under the Minsk agreements are crystal clear and again the choice is Russia's. As the President has said, we'll judge Russia by its actions, not its words. The United States will start rolling back sanctions on Russia only when the Minsk agreements are fully implemented.

But the reverse is also true. We have already begun consultations with our European partners on further sanctions pressure should Russia continue fueling the fire in the east or other parts of Ukraine, fail to implement Minsk or grab more land as we saw in Debaltseve.

Mr. Chairman, members of this committee, America's investment in Ukraine is about far more than protecting the choice of a single European country. It's about protecting the rules-based system across Europe and globally. It's about saying ''no'' to borders changed by force, and to big countries intimidating their neighbors or demanding spheres of influence. It's about protecting our 25 year American investment in the prospect of a Europe whole, free, and at peace and the example that sets for nations and people around the world who want more democratic, prosperous futures.

I thank this committee for its bipartisan support and commitment.

The CHAIRMAN. Thank you.
Mr. McKeon.

## STATEMENT OF HON. BRIAN P. McKEON, PRINCIPAL DEPUTY UNDER SECRETARY OF DEFENSE FOR POLICY, U.S. DEPARTMENT OF DEFENSE, WASHINGTON, DC

Mr. McKEON. Thank you very much, Mr. Chairman and Senator Menendez. I appreciate the opportunity to appear before you today.

Having spent nearly half of my professional life on the staff of this committee under then-Senator Biden, it feels good to be back in this room, although a little daunting to be on this side of the witness table.

The statement I have submitted to the committee, which I will now summarize, is on behalf of myself and Admiral Pandolfe. So we will save a little time on the back end.

I will not repeat the state of play on the Minsk agreement, which Assistant Secretary Nuland has just summarized.

Since the beginning of this crisis, the United States has vigorously pursued a multipronged approach in response to Russia's aggression in Ukraine. We have raised the cost to Russia for its actions, reassured allies of our unwavering support to their security, and provided tangible support to Ukraine to help it through the crisis.

Working closely with Europe and other partners and allies, the administration has imposed real costs on Russia for its aggressive actions. The Department of Defense has halted defense and military cooperation with Russia. The administration has also prohibited exports of sensitive technologies that could be used in Russia's military modernization, has imposed blocking sanctions on 18 Russian defense technology firms.

Second, we are taking visible, concrete measures to reassure our allies and partners in Europe, and to deter further Russian aggression. Thanks to Congress, the European Reassurance Initiative, or

ERI, is helping the Department to increase and sustain an enhanced United States air, sea, and ground presence in Europe and to improve facilities needed to reinforce allies along the border with Russia. Additionally, ERI funds will be used to bolster our assistance to Ukraine and to the Baltic partners.

As part of our reassurance measures, we have maintained a persistent presence of U.S. military forces in each of the Baltic States, Poland, and the Black Sea since April of last year. We have also had a near persistent presence in Romania and Bulgaria. We have tripled the number of United States aircraft taking part in our Baltic air policing rotation, provided refueling aircraft for NATO Airborne Warning and Control System missions, deployed U.S. Navy ships to the Black and Baltic Seas 14 times, and increased training flights in Poland.

In the coming year, using ERI funds, we will increase our reassurance and deterrence efforts with additional measures, which are detailed in my prepared statement.

Similarly, NATO has taken concrete steps to reassure the allies and to deter Russia. These measures are defensive, proportionate, and fully in line with our obligations under the North Atlantic Treaty to provide for collective defense of the alliance.

Allies have also agreed to measures as part of NATO's readiness action plan that will improve the alliance's long-term military posture and capabilities and ensure it is ready to respond swiftly and firmly to new security challenges. Last month, NATO Defense Ministers decided to enhance the NATO response force by creating a spearhead force, known as a very high readiness joint task force, which will be able to deploy on very short notice. The task force consists of a land component of around 5,000 troops with an appropriate mix of air, maritime, and special operations forces units. It aims to strengthen the alliance's collective defense and ensure that NATO has the right forces in the right place at the right time.

Third, we are providing substantial support to Ukraine as it deals with simultaneous economic and military crises. Ukraine has been a strong partner of the United States and NATO since independence, and our security cooperation with Ukraine dates back to 1992. During this period, the United States provided Ukraine with military training, professional education, communications equipment, and support for border control and counter-proliferation efforts. Unfortunately, the corruption of the Yanukovych regime starved Ukraine's Armed Forces of resources. The neglect of the armed forces by the regime did not, however, strip the military of its professionalism or its determination to fight.

Since the beginning of the crisis, the United States has increased its security assistance to Ukraine. We have committed, as you know, $118 million in material and training assistance to the military, the national guard, and the border guard service. Under ERI in the coming year, we will dedicate at least another $120 million, including $45 million for State Department security assistance programs. Our assistance has been consistent with identified Ukrainian needs and priorities and it is vetted by our country team in Kyiv and a flag-level United States-Ukraine joint commission that continues to assess how to maximize the effect and impact of our assistance. Key areas of assistance include sustainment items, medical support, personal protective gear, secure communications, and perimeter security. We have also provided countermortar radar capabilities, which the Ukrainians tell us they have used to good effect.

Similarly, we are also continuing to conduct longstanding exercises such as Rapid Trident to increase interoperability among Ukraine, the United States, NATO, and Partnership for Peace member nations. The most recent iteration of Rapid Trident last September included a multinational field training exercise and saw the participation of 15 countries and approximately 1,300 personnel.

Other measures remain under active consideration in the administration, including the provision of additional security assistance. As the President has said most recently this weekend, we are looking at all our options, including the possibility of lethal defensive weapons. At the same time, we have made clear we do not believe there is a military solution to the conflict in Ukraine, and we are working actively to support the diplomatic track, as Assistant Secretary Nuland outlined.

In conclusion, Russia's aggressive actions in Ukraine are a threat to the bipartisan objective of American policy since the end of the cold war of seeking a Europe whole, free, and at peace. The United States will continue to work closely with our Ukrainian and European partners to counter these actions and provide reassurance and support to our partners and NATO allies.

Thank you for the opportunity to be here.

[The prepared statement of Mr. McKeon follows:]

PREPARED STATEMENT OF BRIAN P. McKEON

Chairman Corker, Senator Menendez, members of the committee, I appreciate the opportunity to appear before you today.

The crisis in Ukraine continues. After more than a year of aggressive Russian action, the situation in Ukraine remains unstable. As the committee is aware, last year Russia occupied the Crimean Peninsula and subsequently has attempted to annex it. Today, Russia continues its participation and active support to separatists engaged in violence in eastern Ukraine. As Assistant Secretary Nuland informed you, the cease-fire under the terms of the Minsk Implementation Plan may be holding in many areas of eastern Ukraine, and we have seen some progress on withdrawals of weapons. However, cease-fire violations continue, almost all of them on the Russian and separatist side; this is not an ''immediate and comprehensive cease-fire'' as called for by the plan. We remain concerned that this may be a period of strategic pause—a stalling tactic as a precursor to more violence as occurred before the most recent Russian and separatist assault in January. We call on Russia to stop ''moving the goalposts,'' to uphold the cease-fire, and to allow Ukraine the freedom to choose its own path.

As you heard from Assistant Secretary Nuland, since the beginning of the crisis the United States has vigorously pursued a multipronged approach in response to Russia's aggression in Ukraine. We have raised the costs to Russia for its actions, reassured allies of our unwavering support to their security, and provided tangible support to Ukraine to help it through the crisis. I wish to highlight the measures taken in each of these three areas, including actions taken by the Department of Defense.

RAISING COSTS TO RUSSIA

First, working closely with Europe and other partners and allies, the administration has imposed real costs on Russia for its aggressive actions. We have worked diligently to isolate Russia at the United Nations Security Council, we and our partners have suspended Russia's participation in the G–8. The Department of Defense halted defense and military cooperation with Russia. The administration has also prohibited exports of sensitive technologies that could be used in Russia's military modernization and has imposed blocking sanctions on 18 Russian defense technology firms. Most important, the United States and its European allies have imposed a series of sanctions to raise the costs for Russia and Ukrainian separatists for their aggressive actions, including targeted sectoral sanctions in the Russian finance, energy, and defense sectors, which have had a substantial impact on Russia's economy.

## REASSURING ALLIES

Second, we are taking visible, concrete measures to reassure our allies and partners in Europe and to deter further Russian aggression. Thanks to Congress, the European Reassurance Initiative, or ERI, is helping the Department to increase and sustain an enhanced U.S. air, sea, and ground presence in Europe and to improve facilities needed to reinforce allies along the border with Russia. Additionally, ERI funds will be used to bolster our assistance to Ukraine and to the Baltic allies.

As part of our reassurance measures, we have maintained a persistent presence of U.S. military forces in each of the Baltic States, Poland, and the Black Sea since April 2014. We tripled the number of U.S. aircraft taking part in our Baltic Air Policing rotation, provided refueling aircraft for NATO Airborne Warning and Control System missions, deployed U.S. Navy ships to the Black and Baltic Seas 14 times, and increased training flights in Poland.

In 2015, using ERI funds, the United States will increase its reassurance and deterrence efforts with additional measures, including:

- Rotating an armored brigade to Europe for several months;
- Prepositioning in Europe a second battalion-sized set of tanks and Bradley fighting vehicles;
- Conducting additional bilateral and multilateral exercises and training with allies and partners;
- Deploying a squadron of U.S. Air Force A–10s to Europe for nearly 6 months;
- Making infrastructure improvements to eight airfields;
- Prepositioning fuel and ammunition; and,
- Building the capacity of close partners such as Georgia, Moldova, and Ukraine to enhance interoperability to work alongside U.S. and NATO forces, as well as to provide for their own defense.

Similarly, NATO has taken concrete steps to reassure allies and deter Russia. These measures are defensive, proportionate, and fully in line with the obligations under the North Atlantic Treaty to provide for allied defense. NATO's deterrence measures have included:

- Increasing the number of aircraft on air-policing patrols over the Baltics and the number of bases used for Baltic Air Policing;
- Deploying aircraft to Bulgaria, Poland, and Romania for training and exercises;
- Commencing AWACS surveillance flights over the territory of our eastern allies;
- Sending more ships to patrol the Baltic Sea, the Black Sea, and the Mediterranean;
- Deploying ground troops to the eastern parts of the alliance for training and exercises, on a rotational basis; and,
- Conducting over 200 NATO and national exercises in Europe in 2014.

Allies have also agreed to measures as part of NATO's Readiness Action Plan that will improve the alliance's long-term military posture and capabilities, and ensure it is ready to respond swiftly and firmly to new security challenges. NATO Defense Ministers in February decided to enhance the NATO Response Force by creating a "spearhead force," known as a Very High Readiness Joint Task Force (VJTF), that will be able to deploy at very short notice. The VJTF consists of a land component of around 5,000 troops with an appropriate mix air, maritime, and SOF units. It aims to strengthen the alliance's collective defense and ensure that NATO has the right forces in the right place at the right time.

## EFFORTS TO SUPPORT UKRAINE

Third, we are providing substantial support to Ukraine as it deals with simultaneous economic and military crises. Ukraine has been a strong partner to the United States and NATO since its independence, and our security cooperation with Ukraine dates back to 1992. Such cooperation over the past two decades has paid dividends, as Ukraine has been a steadfast coalition partner in Afghanistan, Iraq, Kosovo, and Bosnia, as well as in counter-piracy operations off the Horn of Africa. During this time, the United States provided Ukraine with military training, professional education, communications equipment, and support for border control and counterproliferation efforts. Unfortunately, the corruption of the Yanukovych regime starved Ukraine's Armed Forces of resources. But the neglect of the Armed Forces by the regime did not strip the military of its professionalism or its determination to fight.

Since the start of the crisis the United States has increased its security-related assistance to Ukraine. We have committed $118 million in material and training assistance to Ukraine's military, National Guard, and Border Guard service. Under ERI, in FY 2015 we will dedicate at least another $120 million including $45 million for State Department security assistance programs. Our assistance has been consistent with identified Ukrainian needs and priorities, and it is vetted by our country team in Ukraine and by a flag-level U.S.-Ukraine Joint Commission that continuously assesses how to maximize the effect and impact of our security assistance. Key areas of material assistance include sustainment items, medical support, personal protective gear, secure communications, and perimeter security. We have also provided countermortar radar capabilities, which the Ukrainians tell us they have used to good effect.

Similarly, we also continue to conduct longstanding exercises such as Rapid Trident to increase interoperability among Ukraine, U.S., NATO, and Partnership for Peace member nations. The most recent Rapid Trident iteration in September 2014 included a multinational field training exercise and saw the participation of 15 countries and approximately 1,300 personnel.

Other measures remain under active consideration in the administration, including the provision of additional security assistance. As the President has said, we are looking at all our options, including the possibility of lethal defensive weapons. At the same time, we have made clear that we do not believe there is a military solution to the conflict in Ukraine, and are working actively to support the diplomatic track.

### CONCLUSION

Russia's aggressive actions in Ukraine are a threat to a bipartisan objective of American policy since the end of the cold war of seeking a Europe whole, free, and at peace. The United States will continue to work closely with our Ukrainian and European partners to counter these actions and to provide reassurance and support to our partners and NATO allies.

Thank you for the opportunity to be here today, and look forward to your questions.

The CHAIRMAN. Thank you.
Mr. Toloui.

## STATEMENT OF HON. RAMIN TOLOUI, ASSISTANT SECRETARY FOR INTERNATIONAL FINANCE, DEPARTMENT OF THE TREASURY, WASHINGTON, DC

Mr. TOLOUI. Chairman Corker, Ranking Member Menendez, and members of the committee, thank you for the opportunity to testify today on the U.S. Government's actions to support Ukraine's economy.

The objective of the United States and international economic assistance strategy toward Ukraine has been to support the efforts of President Poroshenko's government to stabilize, revitalize, and restructure Ukraine's economy. My remarks today will elaborate upon the strategy and its evolution over the past year in response to the conflict in eastern Ukraine. I would note that our efforts to mobilize the international effort to support Ukraine financially have been complemented by the work of others at the Treasury Department to impose costs on Russia for its aggressive actions in Crimea and eastern Ukraine that have exacerbated the challenges facing Ukraine's economy.

Last spring, the United States, together with international partners, supported an international assistance package totaling $27 billion. This assistance centered on a 2-year $17 billion IMF program and also included a $1 billion U.S. loan guarantee and $2.2 billion from the European Union.

The IMF and other donors agree that Ukraine has lived up to its economic reform commitments made in exchange for the support. Over the last year, the Ukrainian Government has initiated steps to reduce the deficit and distortionary natural gas subsidies, improve targeting of social assistance, strengthen the rule of law and reduced corruption, increase transparency within the inefficient state-owned energy company, and initiate financial sector repair. This is very much the comprehensive approach to reform, Chairman Corker, that you referred to. In support of these efforts Treasury advisors are providing the Ukrainian Government with technical assistance.

This was always going to be a challenging program of reform and adjustment. Unfortunately, the intensification of Russian aggression has created significant additional pressure on Ukraine's economy and necessitated further international support to bolster the government's reform efforts. As such, during the past few months, we have mobilized the international community to increase Ukraine's support package by at least $10 billion. Further, the IMF now plans to support Ukraine through the end of 2018 with a larger gross financing package allowing more time for the economy to adjust and for economic reforms to bear fruit.

As part of that international effort, the United States intends to provide a new $1 billion loan guarantee in the first half of 2015, provided Ukraine remains on track with the reform program it has agreed with the IMF. If Ukraine continues making concrete progress on its economic reform agenda and conditions warrant, the U.S. administration will also be willing, working with Congress, to consider providing an additional up to $1 billion loan guarantee in late 2015.

The next step in further driving this augmented international assistance effort is to secure IMF board approval on March 11, tomorrow, for the new IMF program. To meet its reform requirements in advance of the IMF board meeting, the Ukrainian Government has passed meaningful reform measures to improve public financing and reduce inefficient energy subsidies. Provided that the authorities adhere to the reform program and the security situation does not deteriorate further, the IMF projects that Ukraine's economy will expand in 2016 and foreign exchange reserves will rise substantially.

In view of the inherent uncertainties in the security situation, there continue to be risks. This year's intensification of the conflict has imposed severe damage on an already fragile economy. Currency depreciation and deposit flight have put a strain on the banking sector, and significant structural damage has occurred within Ukraine's economy.

Amid these challenges, Ukraine's ambitious reform agenda deserves our continued support. Core United States and global security interests are at stake in Ukraine, and providing economic support to the Ukrainian Government is an essential part of our strategy to respond to Russian aggression. As long as Ukraine's Government continues to undertake difficult reforms, the international community must do all it can to help Ukraine succeed and be prepared to adapt its assistance strategy as required.

At the same time, the international community must continue to ensure that as long as Russia disregards its commitments and fuels violence and instability in Ukraine, the costs for Russia will continue to rise.

Chairman Corker, Ranking Member Menendez, and members of the committee, as with all emerging market crises, our assistance strategy is not without risk, and the path to success is not without obstacles, particularly amid the current security backdrop. However, critical elements needed for success, an ambitious reform program, a government and country committed to change, and a sizable international support package, are currently in place. To that end, we will continue to work closely with our international partners to provide Ukraine the support it needs. The strong backing of Congress has been a critical foundation to these efforts to support Ukraine, and we look forward to working closely together in the months ahead.

And I look forward to answering your questions.

[The prepared statement of Mr. Toloui follows:]

PREPARED STATEMENT OF RAMIN TOLOUI

Chairman Corker, Ranking Member Menendez, and members of the committee, thank you for the opportunity to testify today on the U.S. Government's actions to support Ukraine's economy.

The objective of the United States and international economic assistance strategy toward Ukraine has been to support the efforts of President Poroshenko's government to stabilize, revitalize, and restructure Ukraine's economy. My remarks today will elaborate upon this economic and financial strategy, and its evolution over the past year in response to the conflict in eastern Ukraine. I would note at the outset that our efforts to mobilize the international effort to support Ukraine financially have been complemented by the work of others at the Treasury Department to impose costs on Russia for its aggressive actions in Crimea and eastern Ukraine that have exacerbated the challenges facing Ukraine's economy.

ECONOMIC ASSISTANCE STRATEGY

Last spring, the United States, together with international partners, supported an international assistance package totaling $27 billion. This assistance centered on a 2-year $17 billion International Monetary Fund (IMF) program, and also included a $1 billion U.S. loan guarantee and $2.2 billion from the European Union. In exchange for this support, the Ukrainian authorities committed to an ambitious economic reform agenda to reduce vulnerabilities and increase economic growth potential.

The IMF and other donors agree that Ukraine has lived up to its economic reform commitments. Over the last year, the Ukrainian Government has initiated difficult and urgently needed steps to: reduce the general government deficit; reduce distortionary natural gas subsidies; improve targeting of social assistance to protect the most vulnerable; strengthen the rule of law and reduce corruption; increase transparency within the inefficient state-owned energy company; and initiate financial sector repair. In support of these efforts, Treasury technical advisors are providing the Ukrainian Government with expert assistance in the areas of bank supervision and bank resolution, and government debt and liability management.

This was always going to be a challenging program of reform and adjustment. Unfortunately, the intensification of Russian aggression has created significant additional pressure on Ukraine's economy and necessitated further international support to bolster the government's reform efforts. The fragile security situation has eroded confidence, increased capital outflows, weakened the currency, and depleted foreign exchange reserves. The destruction of economic capacity in eastern Ukraine has driven a deeper and longer economic recession than previously estimated. As such, during the past few months, we have mobilized the international community to increase Ukraine's support package by at least $10 billion. As part of the international effort, the United States intends to provide a new $1 billion loan guarantee in the first half of 2015, provided Ukraine remains on-track with the reform program it has agreed with the IMF. If Ukraine continues making concrete progress on its economic reform agenda and conditions warrant, the U.S. administration will also be willing, working with Congress, to consider providing an additional up to $1 billion loan guarantee in late 2015. As part of this up-sized economic assistance package, the IMF now plans to support Ukraine through end-2018 with a larger gross financing package, allowing more time for the economy to adjust and for economic reforms to bear fruit. Also as part of this package, Ukraine has indicated that it will seek to work with creditors to adjust the profile of its debt to provide additional financial breathing room.

The next step in further driving this augmented international assistance effort is to secure IMF Board approval on March 11 for the new IMF program, which will unlock a large disbursement of IMF financing. Based on international support pledged to date, Ukraine's foreign exchange reserves are set to increase significantly over the next few weeks, which will bolster confidence and provide the authorities with space to further execute their ambitious reform agenda. To meet its reform requirements in advance of the IMF Board meeting, the Ukrainian Government passed meaningful and difficult reform measures to improve public finances and reduce inefficient energy subsidies. Since these measures were taken, Ukraine's currency and capital markets have rebounded significantly. Provided that the authorities adhere to the reform program and the security situation does not deteriorate further, the IMF projects that Ukraine's economy will expand next year and foreign exchange reserves will rise substantially.

In view of the inherent uncertainties in the security situation, there continue to be risks. This year's intensification of the conflict has imposed severe damage on an already fragile economy—particularly the export-oriented regions of eastern Ukraine. Currency depreciation and deposit flight have put a strain on the banking sector, and significant structural damage has occurred within the Ukrainian economy. Overcoming these impacts and restoring market confidence will be challenging.

Amid these challenges, the Ukrainian Government continues to demonstrate a strong commitment to an ambitious reform agenda, and deserves our continued support. Core U.S. and global security interests are at stake in Ukraine, and providing economic support to the Ukrainian Government is an essential part of our strategy to respond to Russian aggression. As long as Ukraine's Government continues to undertake the difficult reforms required to restore economic and financial stability, the international community must do all it can to help Ukraine succeed and be prepared to adapt its assistance strategy as required. And at the same time, the international community must continue to ensure that as long as Russia disregards its commitments and fuels violence and instability in Ukraine, the costs for Russia will continue to rise.

CONCLUSION

Chairman Corker, Ranking Member Menendez, and members of the committee, as with all emerging market crises, our assistance strategy is not without risk and the path to success is not without obstacles, particularly amid the current security backdrop. However, critical elements needed for success—an ambitious reform plan, a government and country committed to change, and a sizable international support package—are currently in place. To that end, we will continue to work closely with the international financial institutions and our partners around the world to provide Ukraine the support it needs and enable Ukraine's people to achieve their economic aspirations. The strong backing of Congress has been a critical foundation to these efforts to support Ukraine, and we look forward to working closely together in the months ahead. I look forward to answering your questions.

The CHAIRMAN. Thank you. We thank each of you for your testimony and Admiral Pandolfe for being here to answer questions.

I will begin with you, Secretary Nuland. I know in the past you have characterized what Russia has done in Ukraine as an invasion. Does that description still stand with you?

Ms. NULAND. We have used that term in the past.

The CHAIRMAN. And are you using that again today?

Ms. NULAND. I am comfortable with that word.

The CHAIRMAN. And just for the record, since Russia does not acknowledge the deaths of their soldiers, if you will, publicly, how many Russian soldiers do you think have been killed in Ukraine as part of this conflict?

Ms. NULAND. Well, Mr. Chairman, as you can imagine, it is pretty difficult to have a completely accurate assessment, given Russia's efforts to mask its dead, but we estimate it is——

The CHAIRMAN. What does our intelligence tell us?

Ms. NULAND [continuing]. In the hundreds and hundreds.

The CHAIRMAN. Hundreds and hundreds? The numbers I thought were substantially higher than that. So under 1,000?

Ms. NULAND. Chairman, I cannot speak to more than 400 or 500 at the moment, but if we have a better number for you in the future, we will come back to you.

The CHAIRMAN. Okay, good.

I know that you have been a strong advocate publicly for support in Ukraine and have been a good person for us to talk to both by phone and here as a witness.

What is the administration's position right now on the Debaltseve as far as what are our demands regarding Russia's, the rebels' withdrawal—from that area and by what timeline?

Ms. NULAND. Well, Mr. Chairman, as you know—and I think it is in my longer statement—we were extremely concerned to see the flattening of Debaltseve after the signing of the Minsk agreement. Debaltseve is outside of the special status territory. So it is territory that the Government of Ukraine did have control of. Under the Minsk agreements, there is supposed to be a complete withdrawal to the lines agreed on September 19. So that would include the vacating of Debaltseve by the separatists.

The CHAIRMAN. So we are demanding that they leave. Is that the U.S. position and by what date?

Ms. NULAND. That is the position that Minsk calls for and we support Minsk, yes.

The CHAIRMAN. And what is that date? What is the timeline by which they have to step back away from Debaltseve?

Ms. NULAND. Well, the implementation agreement of February 12 calls for the full pullback of heavy weapons and military equipment within some 16 days. We are already beyond that, but they are working on it.

With regard to when the——

The CHAIRMAN. They actually are working on it. Russia is working on that?

Ms. NULAND. As I said in my testimony, we have seen incomplete compliance in terms of OSCE access, including in Debaltseve, incomplete compliance in terms of OSCE being able to verify the pullback of separatist heavy weapons. But when you get to the political phase of Minsk, which is to follow this, the political jurisdiction of the special status zone does not include the town of Debaltseve. If the separatists comply, they should be not insisting on having political control of that area by spring.

The CHAIRMAN. Secretary McKeon, we appreciate you coming here today and sitting on that side.

Secretary Carter and Joint Chief Dempsey have both talked about the fact that they would like to see defensive weaponry supported. Secretary Nuland, I know, has advocated for that. We have passed that unanimously out of both Houses, at least passed it unanimously out of the Senate. It came out of the House. There seems to be some debate within the administration, and obviously, the German Ambassador thinks the President has made quiet commitments that we are not going to do that.

What is the status of this debate within the administration where we are all getting mixed signals and very confused by the stance the administration is taking?

Mr. MCKEON. Senator Corker, I cannot speak to what happened in the bilateral meeting between the President and Chancellor Merkel.

The CHAIRMAN. Well, can you speak to where we are in this debate?

Mr. MCKEON. I can. It probably will not be a very satisfying answer, sir. We are still working in the interagency on reviewing a number of options, including lethal defensive weapons, but I cannot give you a timetable on when we might have a decision on additional assistance.

The CHAIRMAN. You said $118 million and other kinds of assistance. But it is my understanding we have committed $118 million or $120 million. We have only delivered half of that. Is that correct?

Mr. MCKEON. About half. That is correct.

The CHAIRMAN. So just for what it is worth, this feels just like 3 years ago the Syrian opposition where basically we were going to help. There were all these things we were going to do. We were going to deliver trucks. They got there way beyond their usefulness.

What is happening? I mean, we have Secretary Nuland come in. She speaks strongly. We see her in Munich. She speaks strongly. We thank her for that. And yet, the administration does not do even what it said it would do. I mean, what is going on with the administration? It is incredibly frustrating for all of us to think the administration truly supports Ukraine; and yet, it feels like they are playing footsy with Russia. There is something else that is happening. They are not really committed to this. And I am wondering if you could speak clearly to what is happening.

Mr. MCKEON. Senator Corker, what I could say is we share your frustration about the speed of delivery of our commitments, and the new Secretary has pressed us on this. In fact, in one of my first meetings with him, he said to us let us start a new policy. Let us not promise assistance unless we can deliver it quickly.

The CHAIRMAN. And what would keep us from being able to deliver $118 million worth of nonlethal assistance?

Mr. MCKEON. It is a range of things, sir. Some, it is a case of finding it in the stocks of the United States military. In the case of some equipment, we are purchasing it off the production line. I can tell you that the head of our Defense Security Cooperation Agency has made this a high priority, and we are pushing him all the time. And the case of the countermortar radars is a good example. We got approval for those in late October, and we got them delivered, trained, and fielded within 2 months. So we are able to move quickly in some instances. In other instances, it is unacceptably slow. But I can assure you we are making it a top priority.

I just cannot explain why in some circumstances it goes slower than we would like.

The CHAIRMAN. And we know this is not your decision. We appreciate you being the messenger. But as Secretary Nuland has said, Russia has invaded Ukraine. We agreed to protect their territorial sovereignty in 1994. They gave up 1,240 nuclear weapons, and we agreed to protect them. And now, as Russia has invaded, we are still not willing to give defensive weapons.

I would just go to Secretary Nuland. Why do you think that is the case? I mean, why would we be so feckless—feckless—in agreeing to something back in 1994 and yet be unwilling to give them the kind of defensive weaponry that they can utilize, not more than they can utilize? Why would we not be doing that? What would be your impression of our inability to make that happen?

Ms. NULAND. Well, Chairman, as Under Secretary McKeon has said, we have provided some significant defensive systems, including the counterfire-mortar radars which have saved lives in Ukraine. We have not answered the entire shopping list from the Ukrainians. There are a lot of factors that go into that. And we are continuing to look at the situation on the ground and the needs and the implementation of Minsk as we evaluate this going forward.

The CHAIRMAN. It is my understanding that we have also dropped back from training the Ukrainian National Guard and put that on hold. Can you just briefly tell me why that is the case, Secretary McKeon?

Mr. MCKEON. Senator Corker, as you know, we had notified your committee I believe several months ago about a program of training for the National Guard. We have not had a decision—never had a decision on the final timing and scope of it. We had talked about doing it this month, but it is still under consideration as to when we would do that training.

The CHAIRMAN. It is pretty evident that we are really not going to do much. It is pretty evident that the strong statements that we have made are statements.

And I will close. I know my time is up.

But I will just say to Mr. Toloui thank you for your presentation. I do hope that we—and our partners—are committed to providing the financial assistance that is going to be necessary to keep Ukraine afloat. I think the greatest victory for Putin—other than certainly making us look really weak to the world right now and certainly not following through on our commitments—I think his greatest victory would be for Ukraine to fall and him not to have to break it—but for it to break by economic conditions there on the ground. And I hope that we are committed. I know others may ask you questions about how much we are committed to provide them.

But thank you all for your testimony. I realize each of you are messengers and not making these decisions.

Secretary Menendez.

Senator MENENDEZ. Well, thanks for the promotion, Mr. Chairman. [Laughter.]

Let me say I am not quite sure why we cannot move ahead. Former National Security Advisor, Dr. Brzezinski, former Secretary of State, Madeleine Albright, both testified before the Senate

Armed Services Committee that the United States should provide defensive weapons to Ukraine. When asked about providing such weapons to Ukraine, Ash Carter said during his confirmation hearing, I very much am inclined in that direction because I think we need to support the Ukrainians in defending themselves. U.S. Army Europe Commander LTG Ben Hodges recently stated his support for providing weapons to Ukraine in order to provide the necessary muscle for a diplomatic solution. The Chairman of the Joint Chiefs of Staff has suggested the same.

So I have a question. Are Dr. Brzezinski, Secretary Albright, Secretary Carter, General Hodges, General Dempsey, and a unanimous Congress all wrong?

Ms. NULAND. I take it that is a question to me, Ranking Member Menendez?

Senator MENENDEZ. Well, either you, Madam Secretary, or the Secretary of the Defense Department, whoever wants to take it. But I mean, you have an overwhelming view from a wide spectrum, and I do not get it. So maybe you can elucidate. Are they all wrong? And if so, why are they wrong?

Ms. NULAND. I think as the interagency discussion on this subject has taught us, there are factors on both sides, and we are continuing to evaluate. I think from where we sit at the State Department, if we can see these Minsk agreements implemented, if we can see peace in eastern Ukraine, that offers the best hope for the Ukrainian people. But we will continue to evaluate the situation as we go forward.

Senator MENENDEZ. Let us stop there. Minsk I, nothing, a disaster. Minsk II only went ahead and largely incorporated more territory that the rebels had taken since Minsk I and made the boundary lines to assure between Ukraine and Russia less capable of actually being pursued because it was all dependent upon some votes on decentralization of the government. There have been, Admiral Pandolfe, about 1,000 violations of the cease-fire. Is that a fair estimate?

Admiral PANDOLFE. I cannot give you a precise figure, but there have been a number.

Senator MENENDEZ. Okay. That is a commonly referred to number, 1,000 violations of the cease-fire.

And so we keep working on this aspirational basis while Russia works effectively to take more and more Ukrainian land. And there is not enough money in the world to be able to help the Ukrainians sustain themselves if they continue to bleed because of the conflict that Russia has created and still stokes in eastern Ukraine.

So I do not get it. Unless you change the calculus for Putin, this is going to continue. He will get his land bridge to Crimea, and so much for our statements about we are not willing to forgive the fact that Crimea is gone. I do not get it.

So I do not know how much the interagency process is going to continue to wait. I guess when all of this is solidified, then it will be too late.

Let me ask you. According to the law, the administration is supposed to report on its plan for increasing military assistance to the Government of Ukraine. It was supposed to have done that by February the 15th. It has not. What day can we expect this report to be submitted?

Ms. NULAND. Senator Menendez, we very much regret that these reports are not yet ready. We are continuing to work on some of the programmatic issues that we want to reflect in these reports, including those that flow from our 2015 budget, and speaking for us, we have only just had our pass-back. So we are hoping to have them up to you in coming weeks if not in coming days.

Senator MENENDEZ. Secretary McKeon, welcome back to the committee. You did a lot of distinguished work here while you were here.

On December 10, you testified before the Armed Services Subcommittee that the United States was considering a variety of military responses to Russia's violation of the INF Treaty. Among the responses you outlined was the placement of U.S. ground-launched cruise missiles in Europe, which I assume would have nuclear capability. Can you further elaborate on the military responses the administration is considering to Russia's INF violation and how NATO allies have reacted to the suggestion of the introduction of U.S. GLCM's?

Mr. MCKEON. Senator Menendez, on the last issue, when I talked about that in the hearing, it was in the hypothetical sense. Introducing a GLCM into Europe would not be in compliance with the treaty. So we would have, in the first instance, to withdraw from the treaty or declare it null and void based on Russia's actions. I had put that out there as just something we obviously could do if we chose to come out of the treaty.

What we are looking at in terms of options, countermeasures, some of which are compliant with the treaty, some of which would not be—I can describe a range of things in different buckets. One would be defenses of NATO sites or U.S. sites in Europe. Second would be counterforce capabilities to prevent attacks, and third would be countervailing strike capabilities to go after other Russian targets. So we are looking at a range of things.

We are still, in the first instance, trying to persuade Russia to come back into compliance with the treaty and remember why they signed it in the first instance. But if that does not succeed, our objective is to ensure they have no significant military advantage from their violation of the treaty.

Senator MENENDEZ. And so far, we have not succeeded at getting them back into compliance.

Mr. MCKEON. That is correct.

Senator MENENDEZ. Now let me ask you Secretary Toloui. At the height of the Maidan protests in December 2013, Russia extended a $3 billion bond in an attempt to keep President Yanukovych in power. He fled the country with unknown millions, but Ukraine and its citizens retained the debt. Given the exorbitant terms of the bond, Russia can demand immediate repayment in full, and if Ukraine refuses to pay, it would trigger default on all Ukrainian debt. In my estimation, that is clearly an economic weapon.

Now there is precedent for shielding countries from this type of coercion. In 2003, the United States and the EU, among others, adopted in their legal systems U.N. Security Council Resolution 1483, which made Iraqi oil and gas assets immune to seizure by private creditors. The U.K. Parliament could similarly enact legislation to deny enforcement of the bond since it is governed under English law.

If Russia refuses to reschedule payments on the bond or reclassify it as a government-to-government debt under the auspices of the Paris Club, has the administration engaged with the British Government on the possibility of denying enforcement of the bond under British law?

Mr. TOLOUI. Ranking Member Menendez, thank you for that question. I think you touched on a few points, so let me touch on a few aspects that are relevant.

First of all, Russia has not asked for, has not demanded, so-called acceleration of this payment.

In addition, the Ukrainian Government, in the context of its IMF program, has indicated that it intends to discuss with creditors, which would include Russia, the rescheduling of obligations falling due, primarily within the scope of the IMF program. That would include this Russian $3 billion. And those discussions are only beginning with what we anticipate will be the approval of the IMF program tomorrow.

Second, let me also mention that Treasury, specifically our FinCEN, is cooperating with the Ukrainian authorities on the other issue that you mentioned which is the recovery of assets that went missing with the departure of the previous regime.

So we are certainly willing to look at the issue that you mentioned, should that eventuality arise, but right now, as I said, Russia has not accelerated this claim, and also this claim is going to be subject to the discussions between the Ukrainian Government and its creditors.

Senator MENENDEZ. Well, one final point. I hope we do not wait until Russia pulls such a trigger. I hope they do not. But then if it is all too late and the process of doing what is necessary to create the appropriate protection under international law, as it relates to the U.N. Security Council resolutions, may be too late. So it seems to me there is no harm in having a discussion to be poised for that possibility so that we are not on the back end of trying to play catchup ball.

Thank you, Mr. Chairman.

The CHAIRMAN. Thank you, Senator.

Senator Gardner.

Senator GARDNER. Thank you, Mr. Chairman, for this hearing today, and thank you to the witnesses for testifying today.

I am going to start with Secretary Nuland and just talk briefly about some of the comments that were made last week at a hearing the committee held, including witnesses, Gary Kasparov, as well as President Saakashvili. When I asked the President about his role with Ukraine and to talk about the promises that he believes have been made by the United States to Ukraine and whether or not we had met those promises, I think the answer was clearly he did not feel that we had lived up to all that we had promised. And the bargain that the United States had entered into—excuse me—the agreement—the benefits of the bargain they had not yet received in terms of promises of our commitment to them.

In your testimony, you stated that the United States must keep faith with Ukraine. How do you mesh his belief through his representation of Ukraine and your statement that we have kept faith with the people of Ukraine?

Ms. NULAND. Well, I cannot speak to how former Georgian President Saakashvili comes to his conclusion, but I would simply say that I think this Congress has been enormously generous and responsive to the administration's request, including going above and beyond in some cases the requests that we have made, including in the category of the European Reassurance Initiative where we have more money for Ukraine than we asked for.

What we have been trying to do, both through the loan guarantee program and through the bilateral assistance that I outlined in some detail, is to try to support the implementation of these very, very tough reforms that the Ukrainians are making, and we will continue to do that.

We have also fielded a huge number of technical advisors into the ministries to help them both with the drafting of legislation and with the implementation.

And on the security assistance side, the numbers are significant as compared to previous support for Ukraine, but as Under Secretary McKeon said, we want to see it move faster.

Senator GARDNER. And thank you.

And I believe this question is probably more appropriate to Mr. McKeon, as you discussed in your comments to the chairman, according to an Associated Press article, the German Ambassador claimed that President Obama agreed not to send arms to Ukraine. What is the administration's current posture on lethal assistance to Ukraine?

Mr. McKEON. Senator, we are still reviewing it. It is still an option.

Senator GARDNER. And when do you believe this review will be completed?

Mr. McKEON. I hope soon but I cannot put a timetable on it.

Senator GARDNER. Soon. Is that days, weeks, months?

Mr. McKEON. I hesitate to predict, sir.

Senator GARDNER. What has your conversation been with the Ukraine leadership regarding this assistance?

Mr. McKEON. There are conversations going all the time in the field with Ambassador Pyatt but also my former boss, the Vice President, has put President Poroshenko and the Prime Minister on speed dial. He talks to them at least once a week it seems. I do not know the latest of what he has said to them on this issue. I think in general they are getting the same information that I am giving you, that it is under consideration.

Senator GARDNER. So they would say the same thing to you as well, that they have not heard. They do not know when this assistance——

Mr. McKEON. That is correct. And they have made their requests and interests known. There is no doubt about that.

Senator GARDNER. When we are talking about the cease-fire and the Russia-backed offensive, do you think—in your intelligence, your reports that you have seen, how much time do we have before Putin renews his push into Ukraine? Mr. McKeon?

Mr. McKEON. Sir, getting inside President Putin's head and predicting his next move is an ongoing challenge for the intelligence community, as well as the policy community. I can tell you some reporting today that I can give you on an unclassified basis, some of which Assistant Secretary Nuland gave briefly in her testimony. The Russians continue to operate in eastern Ukraine where they are providing command and control support, operating air defense systems, and fighting alongside the separatists. As she said, they are moving military equipment, and there are still battalion tactical groups across the border of some significant number. But when they may make another move I do not think anybody can say.

Senator GARDNER. In terms of sanctions, you mentioned sanctions, Secretary Nuland. What are we doing right now in terms of the European Union governments such as Hungary, Greece, Cyprus, those nations who have been opposed to traditional sanctions on Russia—what have we been doing to talk to them about the steps needed and necessary for additional sanctions?

Ms. NULAND. Well, despite some publicly stated concerns, those countries that you mentioned have supported sanctions in the council when the leaders come together. We continue to talk to them bilaterally about these issues. I will make another trip out to some of those countries in the coming days and weeks.

But we are also working with the commission itself to continue to design sanctions that if we need to use them, if they need to be applied either in deterrent or actual, have more of an effect on Russia than they do on the European economy or our own economy. So that is part of the conversation that we have.

Senator GARDNER. In that consideration of design of sanctions, does the administration support and what have the conversations been expelling Russia from the SWIFT financial system?

Mr. TOLOUI. I think it would be better not to get into the details of potential actions that we could take. The framework that we evaluate all potential actions is basically the impact that they would have on Russia and the Russian economy against the spillover or blowback that would occur both to the United States and our partners in Europe. So without commenting on specific actions, that would be the prism through which we would be evaluating something like that.

Senator GARDNER. But you have discussed the SWIFT financial system option with European counterparts?

Mr. TOLOUI. We have discussed a whole range of options for further sanctions.

Senator GARDNER. Mr. McKeon, last week we also talked about the length of time it would take for NATO to train a capable Ukrainian military that can successfully defend its territory. What time length do you think it would take? How much time do you think it would take to train Ukrainian military forces?

Mr. McKEON. Well, Senator, it depends on the type of training and the scope of training, how many units we were talking about. The training that the chairman asked me about that was on the books is being looked at for the National Guard Forces was going to be over the course of 6 months, and I think it was five or six companies or battalions. But, Frank, do you know the details on that?

Admiral PANDOLFE. Four.

Mr. McKEON. So if we were to train all of their military—you are talking over 100,000 people—that would take a much longer period of time, sir.

Senator GARDNER. Thank you, Mr. Chairman.

The CHAIRMAN. Secretary Shaheen? I am having trouble with all these Secretaries, and you all could serve extremely well in those positions. I apologize for the demotion. [Laughter.]

Senator SHAHEEN. Well, thank you, Senator Corker. I appreciate that.

And thank you to all of our witnesses for being here today.

I want to begin by just sharing the frustration that we have heard from other members of this committee about the slowness with which we are providing assistance to Ukraine on the weapons side, not just about the decision, which seems to be taking a very long time on providing assistance, but the other forms of assistance that would be helpful to the Ukrainian military that is in the field.

I had an opportunity to meet last week with some representatives from Ukraine, a member of Parliament and some others. And one of the things they talked about was—and I got into a back and forth with them about the reservations that have been expressed by this administration and by Chancellor Merkel and other Europeans about providing weapons and the extent to which that might escalate the conflict. And they said a couple of things that really resonated with me.

One was that they were not sure that the conflict could be escalated to much worse than they expect it to be, in fact, under the current circumstances, and that there was a real symbolic impact should we provide defensive weapons that would have a real morale boost on both the military and on the people of Ukraine.

So in our analysis of the pros and cons of providing defensive assistance, do we disagree with that assessment, that there would be a real symbolic impact to providing that help? I guess this is directed at either you, Secretary Nuland, or Brian McKeon.

Mr. McKEON. Senator, all of our assistance to the Ukrainians is providing not just symbolic but real assistance to support their government across the board, both economic and the security assistance. So I am not going to deny that any assistance we provide would be of importance to the Ukrainians.

What I would say, though, about what we have already provided and what we have committed is it is meeting real Ukrainian military needs. The armed forces were somewhat stripped bare by the corruption of the last regime, and so while I realize a lot of it seems rather basic in terms of——

Senator SHAHEEN. No, I appreciate that, and I am not disagreeing with that at all. I am expressing my frustration, as others have, with the timeliness of providing that assistance, as well as a decision about whether we are going to, in fact, provide defensive weapons.

And I guess I would ask this of you, Secretary Nuland. Do we think there is a point at which Chancellor Merkel would feel like the second Minsk agreement has failed and that an effort to find a peaceful resolution to the conflict has failed and therefore we may need to think about other steps?

Ms. NULAND. Senator, we are in an intense conversation with our allies about a common standard for measuring implementation with Minsk and ensuring that the OSCE gives us all, whether it is Chancellor Merkel, President Obama, or anybody else, a clear picture of where the cease-fire is holding, where it is not, where OSCE has access, where it does not, where weapons are being pulled back so that we can measure.

We have talked with our European allies, including Germany, about two things, not only seeing those things implemented but also about the danger of any future land grab, which is why I shouted out this village of Shyrokyne which is on the road to Mariupol.

But there is now this third concern that I also mentioned in my opening, which is the continued resupply over the border which is not compatible with either the spirit or the letter of Minsk. So we need to watch all of those things together. As I said, sanctions are going to have to increase. Pressure is going to have to increase if Minsk is not implemented.

Senator SHAHEEN. Well, as I know you all know, there was a European Subcommittee hearing last week on Ukraine, and one of the concerns that was expressed was about the economic assistance because if the economy of Ukraine fails, then a resolution to the conflict probably is moot.

But one concern that we discussed was the ability of the Ukrainian people to continue to support the reforms that are being enacted. And I wonder if you could speak to that, Secretary Nuland.

Ms. NULAND. Well, thank you, Senator. This is a real concern for Ukraine's leaders, whether they are in the executive or they are in the Rada. As I outlined in my opening, the kinds of intensive changes to the structure of the economy are going to have impacts in people's pocketbooks and in people's lives, including the raising of the pension age, increased energy prices. So this is why we are working so hard with the IMF and our international partners that as Ukraine takes these tough measures, that the support comes in quickly so that the economy can stabilize, so investment can come back, so that the people can see a light at the end of the tunnel. We have to get Ukraine growing again.

Senator SHAHEEN. Thank you.

One of the other things that was mentioned at last week's hearing—and I guess this question is probably for you, Admiral Pandolfe—and that is the concern that Putin might try to test the Article 5 commitment of NATO countries. And can you talk about what steps we are taking to try and deter Putin from thinking that he should test that?

Admiral PANDOLFE. Well, yes, ma'am.

First of all, our commitment to Article 5 is ironclad, as is all the allies, and that needs to be understood—and we believe that is understood—to emphasize that NATO has enacted some reassurance measures, which include increasing air, ground, and sea forces in the eastern parts of Europe. They are also adapting their force structure with a very high readiness joint task force and standing up what is called NATO force integration units to facilitate the flow of reinforcements, should that be needed, into eastern Europe. These all come out of the Wales Conference. So it is a head of state-level commitment, and NATO is moving forward with that.

And on the United States side, the ERI monies that were authorized by the Congress are most appreciated and are very much helping in that as well.

Senator SHAHEEN. Thank you.

Thank you, Mr. Chairman.

The CHAIRMAN. Senator Perdue, please.

Senator PERDUE. Thank you, Mr. Chairman.

I just want to echo the frustration that you are hearing this morning. Because of the intransigence of this administration, it seems to me that all of a sudden we are in an era where our allies do not trust us and our enemies do not fear us. You know, as it was mentioned earlier, Ukraine unilaterally gave up over 1,000 nuclear weapons on the assurance that their national security would be protected. NATO and the United States was behind that.

Last September, with President Poroshenko by his side, President Obama promised to help Ukraine build up an effective security force to defend themselves from aggression. And yet, here we are today talking about more delays in terms of getting that support.

Kurt Volcker, a former U.S. Ambassador to NATO, has written that this new cease-fire amounts to, ''an institutionalization of a frozen conflict inside Ukraine along the lines of Abkhazia and South Ossetia in Georgia and Transnistria and Moldova. This is exactly what the Kremlin wants.''

Admiral, I have just got a couple questions. Do you think that Putin's objective is to create a frozen conflict like the ones in Georgia and Moldova? And if so, what would be our response to that?

Admiral PANDOLFE. Senator, I think his objective is to keep Ukraine destabilized so it does not effectively join the West. He is threatened by progressive democracies on his borders in my opinion, and he is trying everything he can to prevent that from happening.

In their previous responses, Secretary Nuland and Secretary McKeon have pointed out that we have implemented a wide array of initiatives focused on generating pressure, economic, diplomatic, and military, to try to force the Russians to stop this behavior and respect the territorial integrity of Ukraine.

Senator PERDUE. Thank you.

And from a strategic perspective, in recent months Russia has kidnapped an Estonian intelligence officer on Estonian soil, warned Latvia of unfortunate consequences for its alleged mistreatment of ethnic Russians, forced Sweden to reroute a civilian airliner recently to prevent a collision with a Russian military jet, and flown strategic bombers over the English Channel actually, and sent unannounced formations of military aircraft into European airspace.

I would like to follow up on Senator Shaheen's question about Article 5. But do you believe Putin's strategic objective is to undermine the credibility of NATO's guarantee to secure all its member states?

Admiral PANDOLFE. I do. I think President Putin would like very much to undermine the NATO alliance, and we are working very hard to communicate to him the solidarity of that alliance and taking steps to emphasize and illustrate that solidarity.

Senator PERDUE. Can you talk specifically about what is being done by NATO in Estonia, Latvia, and Lithuania in regard to that?

Admiral PANDOLFE. Well, as mentioned a moment ago, the reassurance measures being taken by NATO do include—and the United States is part of this obviously—rotating forces through the Baltic States, engaging those states in terms of exercises and training and assistance, as well as facilitating additional aircraft being stationed into those countries. NATO AWACS are flying over eastern Europe to a greater extent. Ships are in the Baltic and the Black Seas to a greater extent. All of this holistically is designed to bolster and underline the Article 5 commitments.

Senator PERDUE. Thank you.

And one last question, Secretary Toloui. All four of you have said in different ways that the solution here is diplomatic, economic, and military. My question is on the sanctions. You know, Russia does not have a consumer economy. They have got an energy economy. Their banking sector can be hit and also their military arms manufacturing sector.

Can you speak in a nonclassified way about what needs to be done from the sanctions perspective that can actually get his attention at this point?

Mr. TOLOUI. Senator Perdue, thank you for that question.

The sectors that you mentioned actually have been targeted through the sanctions. Both the defense sector and the financial sector have been subject not only to what we call sectoral sanctions, which restricts the ability of companies in that sector to borrow money, to tap the capital markets, which are needed for them to develop their businesses, but also in particular in the defense sector, there have been individual companies listed and subject to asset freezes.

So those sectors are very important. They are part of the reason why the sanctions have had the effect that they have had on the Russian economy with the currency depreciating by more than 40 percent, the economy expected to contract this year, inflation rising to over 17 percent. So those sectors are very important. They have been part of our tailored sanctions program, and these are the effects that we have seen.

Senator PERDUE. Thank you, Mr. Chairman.

The CHAIRMAN. Senator Murphy.

Senator MURPHY. Thank you very much, Mr. Chairman.

Thank you to the panel for being here today. I would just note to the chairman and ranking member, Senator McCain was in Connecticut yesterday, and we held a townhall meeting with Connecticut's Ukrainian American population. We had an overflow crowd at the Ukrainian National Home in Hartford, probably around 300–400 people. And they raised some of the similar concerns that were raised here today, but they also expressed real and heartfelt appreciation for the fact that if it were not for the leadership of the United States rallying the international community to the economic assistance that is allowed for the Ukrainian Government to still stand, if it was not for our leadership on rallying the international community towards a policy of sanctions, this story would have played out in a very different way. This is a dire situation in eastern Ukraine today, but I think many of the people that I represent, though they want us to go further, understand what we have done thus far and its importance to the ability of Ukraine to continue to defend itself to the degree that it can.

I have one specific question, and then I wanted to talk a little bit about some of the concerns that many of us have about a policy of providing defensive arms, though I support it.

First is the question of what the Budapest Memorandum obligates the United States to do. Already today I have heard some of my colleagues talk about the Budapest Memorandum as obligating the United States to defend or obligating NATO to defend Ukraine from a territorial attack. I think it is important for us to know exactly what we are obligated to do when we sign these international agreements, notwithstanding our unanimity in our belief that we think we should provide defensive weapons to the Ukrainians.

So maybe I will pose this question to you, Secretary Nuland. It is my understanding the Budapest Memorandum obligates each country individually to respect the territorial integrity of Ukraine but, significantly, is not a mutual defense treaty, does not obligate any of those countries to then defend Ukraine. It is not comparable to Article 5. I just think it is important for us to understand if that is actually the case.

Ms. NULAND. First of all, Senator, as a native Connecticut girl, I am glad to see that Connecticut Ukrainian Americans are active and supportive of Ukraine.

I was part of the negotiating team that worked on the Budapest Memorandum, so I know it well. You are accurate. It was a political agreement among the four signatories, notably the United States, the United Kingdom, the Russian Federation, and Ukraine, to respect the sovereignty and territorial integrity of Ukraine, not to attack her. But it was a political agreement. It did not have legally binding treaty force or legally binding national defense obligations.

That said, it is Russia that has violated the spirit and the letter of that agreement.

Senator MURPHY. Agreed.

Mr. McKeon, I want to just talk a little bit about how circumstances on the ground would play out in the event that we decided to give substantial defensive weapons to the Ukrainians. The supposition is that Putin is not paying a big enough price simply with economic sanctions, and that the price that he would pay perhaps in greater numbers of lives lost that he would not be able to cloak in secrecy due to increased U.S. assistance would change his calculus. I think that is a chance worth taking. That is why I have joined with my colleagues in supporting providing defensive weapons. But I understand that it is a chance and that there is also a significant chance that that is not how things will go, that he will just continue his march straight through the lines that we have fortified.

I do not know if you are to this point in terms of your thinking or the proposals that you have been making to the President, to the Secretary, but what would we do in the event that we provided a certain level of defensive weaponry, Putin amassed additional forces, moved straight through the lines that we have then supplied? Would we be in the position of then having to send additional supplies, additional weapons? How does this play out in the case that it does not go the way that we hope it goes whereby Putin pays a bigger price than he is paying today, stops his aggression, or comes to the table? What happens if that does not work?

Mr. MCKEON. Senator Murphy, without getting into all the specifics of the internal debate in the administration, in some respects you have put your finger on the conundrum. From the beginning of this crisis, we have looked at ways to increase the costs on President Putin, to deter further aggression, and to change his calculus. And so that is certainly part of the thinking that goes into weighing whether additional weapons, including lethal defensive weapons, would achieve that and then on the opposite side what you said about does this raise the ante. I do not want to say does this provoke him because he does not need any provoking. Then what would Ukraine feel that the United States owes them in terms of additional assistance? So it is trying to see to the second, third, and fourth move on this chessboard that is part of the conversation.

Senator MURPHY. Yes, I agree with you. I do not buy this argument that us supplying the Ukrainians with defensive weapons is going to provoke Putin. He has got a plan here that he is going to carry out regardless. We are already in for a pretty significant commitment as it is. I just want to make sure—and I think you are suggesting that you are having these conversations—that we are playing this out not just to step one, but to step two and three and four. I think very often we supply you with advice that does not necessarily contemplate the follow-on actions of our initial commitment.

A very final question. I will try to make it quick. Back to you, Secretary Nuland. Just speak to us about the greater challenge here. We are seeing the tip of the iceberg when it comes to the tools that Russia is using, and frankly you and our Government, writ large, is vastly underresourced to try to prevent the next Ukraine from occurring. And as I have been saying a number of times in a number of different forums, at the same time that we are debating the assistance that we should be giving to Ukraine, we really need to be having a discussion about how we resource State and Defense to help all these other countries that we are talking about, whether it be the Baltics, the Balkans, Moldova, Georgia, to try to make sure that this is the last crisis of this proportion that we face in the region.

Ms. NULAND. Thank you, Senator, and thank you for your attention to some of the underresourced parts of Europe, in particular the Balkans and Central Europe.

Well, as you said, in addition to the security challenges and not only the security challenges in Ukraine and the other key periphery states like Moldova and Georgia, but also to the alliance itself as Under Secretary McKeon and Admiral Pandolfe have spoken to, there are all kinds of asymmetric challenges posed by this conflict, whether you are talking about the use of energy as a weapon, which requires us to work much more intensively with the EU and with our European allies and partners on energy diversification, the work that we have been doing on reverse flow gas to Ukraine, more LNG terminals in the Baltics, now looking at the energy dependence of some of our allies in southern Europe. We would like to be able to do more to help Bulgaria, Hungary, Croatia, and other countries like that, although we are doing a lot together with the EU.

Things like use of corruption as a tool of malign influence to undermine sovereignty, whether you are talking about directly paying political candidates or whether you are talking about just ensuring that there is enough dirty money in the system to undercut democratic institutions or to make individual political actors vulnerable to outside pressure. So we are working with countries to expose that and also to close the space for corruption in their system particularly focused on central Europe and the Balkans.

The propaganda, which is not simply what you see in terms of news, but it is also under-the-table efforts to support what looked like legitimate NGOs but are actually agents of influence in countries that change the debate on things that we are working on, whether it is about TTIP or whether it is about Ukraine or other things. So there is a lot to focus on, particularly in the Balkans, where they are not, most of them, cemented into the alliance, and many of them not cemented into the EU, so they are more at risk, but also in allied territory.

Senator MURPHY. Thank you, Mr. Chairman.

The CHAIRMAN. Before turning to Senator Johnson, I do want to say that countries watching the last exchange—Madam Secretary, from a person who helped write the Budapest agreement, apparently it was a superficial agreement, only a political agreement. I would say that countries watching that last exchange would be pretty reticent to come to any agreement with the United States for sure, the U.K., and Russia regarding nuclear arms. My guess is that last exchange would be a pretty major setback to anyone who thought we were ever serious about an agreement relative to nuclear proliferation.

But with that, I will turn it over to Senator Johnson.

Senator JOHNSON. Thank you, Mr. Chairman. Yes, that answer to that question certainly does not reassure the allies, which I think was one of the phrases I heard in the testimony.

Senator Gardner and Senator Shaheen mentioned the hearing we had last week in our European subcommittee. I called that hearing to try to lay out and describe reality, to really tell the story of what Russia has become under Vladimir Putin. I would refer people to my written opening remarks where we laid out a pretty revealing timeline that included 29 political assassinations. And of course, the day after we called the hearing, we saw the assassination of Boris Nemtsov. Pretty stark.

I want to talk about the strategy here. We have talked about the objectives of Vladimir Putin. I want to talk about the strategy. During that hearing, Gary Kasparov, who has been a leading voice of the opposition, said that Putin rebuilt a police state in Russia in full view of the outside world, and now he is confident enough in his power to attempt to export that police state abroad to Georgia, to Ukraine, to Moldova. Where next?

Former Georgia President Saakashvili told our subcommittee that only the swift and immediate action of the U.S. Government to train and equip the Ukrainians can stop Putin's strategy to deconstruct the transatlantic architecture, to deconstruct the post-cold-war order.

Secretary Nuland, do you agree that that is by and large what Vladimir Putin is trying to do? And if you do not agree, what is his strategy? What is his overall motivation? What is his overall goal?

Ms. NULAND. Well, I certainly agree with the way Admiral Pandolfe characterized his motives earlier in this hearing. He is looking to keep countries in the former Soviet space under his political and economic control. He is looking to roll back the gains of a Europe whole, free, and at peace, which is why all of the things that we are talking about here, whether it is allied reassurance and making sure that where we do have treaty commitments, which is to our NATO allies, that every millimeter of space is defended, but also to help strengthen and provide more resilience, political security and economic to all the countries in the periphery.

Senator JOHNSON. Earlier in Vladimir Putin's aggression against Ukraine, I heard a number of administration officials saying that we were trying to offer an off-ramp to Vladimir Putin. Does anybody on the panel here believe that Vladimir Putin is looking for an off-ramp? By my evaluation, he is just simply looking for on-ramps, strategically pausing, and looking for that next on-ramp. Anybody want to dispute that?

Mr. McKEON. I do not know that I would call it an off-ramp, Senator. I think there was a point earlier in the crisis where he arguably was. I think, as Admiral Pandolfe said, he is trying to keep Ukraine out of the West and keep it in a destabilized situation. Whether he seeks to go further in Ukraine, I cannot say.

Senator JOHNSON. Certainly from my standpoint, he is really not looking for off-ramps. He is looking for opportunities.

Dr. Stephen Blank testified. I want to see if this is pretty much the administration's evaluation of really what Russia is doing. According to the IHS consultancy firm, Ukrainian authorities, and the Potomac Institute, there are currently 14,400 Russian troops on Ukrainian territory backing up the 29,300 illegally armed formations of separatists in eastern Ukraine. These units are well equipped with the latest main battle tanks, armored personnel carriers, and infantry fighting vehicles plus hundreds of pieces of tube and rocket artillery. There are also 29,400 Russian troops in Crimea and 55,800 amassed along the border with eastern Ukraine.

Is that pretty much this administration's assessment of really what the Russian troop strength is in Crimea and in Ukraine? Whoever is the most qualified.

Mr. McKEON. Senator Johnson, without going into the specifics of the intelligence on the number of Russians in eastern Ukraine, I cannot comment on—it changes from week to week. It is somewhat fluid. Suffice it to say there are many Russian soldiers in eastern Ukraine, and there is no doubt they have transferred hundreds of pieces of equipment.

Senator JOHNSON. You are certainly not saying this assessment is inaccurate. There is a real possibility this is accurate.

Mr. McKEON. I cannot say that the number is exactly right in terms of 14,000. In terms of the numbers on the border, as I mentioned earlier, the latest information we have on the border, there are 11 Russian battalion tactical groups on the Rostov area off of eastern Ukraine.

Senator JOHNSON. Senator Shaheen was talking about meeting with some of the Ukrainian parliamentarians, and I did the same thing. They were certainly concerned about a potential spring offensive by Russia. And, Secretary Nuland, you talked about they are amassing, moving additional heavy equipment into Ukraine. Is that not a big concern?

Ms. NULAND. Senator, that is exactly why we are seeking the greatest degree of fidelity on whether this Minsk agreement is being implemented and strengthening the OSCE so it can give us an accurate picture. But it is also why we are publicly here calling out some of the specific concerns we have, whether it is about the rearming that we have seen in the last couple of days, whether it is about the continued firing in the strategically important villages of Shyrokyne, et cetera. So, again, if Minsk is implemented before spring and things pull back, then that will allow space for politics to begin in eastern Ukraine, but if not, we have to be prepared to have more sanctions pressure on Russia, and that is what we are preparing.

Senator JOHNSON. That is a big "if." I would argue sanctions have not worked particularly well. In one of my meetings with some of our European allies, the comment was made that as Russia becomes weaker economically, they become more dangerous. I kind of agree with that assessment which is again why I believe we have to provide a military response, lethal defensive weaponry.

Let me just close with a quote by Georgian President Saakashvili or certainly his assessment—there are a couple quotes in here— about changing Putin's calculus. As Senator Menendez mentioned, he was there on the front lines when Russia invaded Georgia. In a resolute action on the part of the Bush administration, sending in supplies without Russia really knowing what was on those cargo airplanes, that was certainly one of the factors causing Russia to stop further expansion, aggression into Georgia.

Saakashvili basically said that deployments from Russia's far east are proof that the Kremlin is sensitive to the rising "costs for Putin's invasion of eastern Ukraine" because Russians have "a very thin layer of tolerance for human casualties." So again, that was Saakashvili's assessment, that if we would show some strength, some resolve, in other words, respond to President Poroshenko's plea that, yes, they will provide the courage, they will provide the boots on the ground to fight Vladimir Putin's aggression, but they cannot do it with blankets.

Thank you, Mr. Chairman.

The CHAIRMAN. Senator Cardin.

Senator CARDIN. Thank you very much, Mr. Chairman, and thank you for holding this very important hearing, and I thank all of our witnesses.

There is no question there is strong consensus on this committee, I think in the United States Senate, that the United States needs to do more to help the Ukrainians defend themselves. So I just want to make that clear from the beginning. The Ukrainians need defensive support so they can defend themselves as far as weapons are concerned. And this committee has spoken and many of us have voiced this, and the hearing, I think, has been pretty clear about our position in that regard.

It is also clear that we need to take stronger action against Russia. The tragic assassination of Boris Nemtsov really points out just how extreme the Putin regime has gotten. I think what we could do, Madam Secretary—and I would just urge you to look at—the individuals Mr. Nemtsov exposed who were committing gross violations of Russian rights. It would be appropriate for us to review whether we should be imposing the Magnitsky type sanctions against those individuals that he worked on within Russia.

And let us not forget Nadiya Savchenko who is unlawfully imprisoned in Russia today, who was taken from Ukraine by Russia. This Senate has spoken on Ms. Savchenko through passage of a resolution.

So there is just continued effort, and Russia's violations of its agreements, including the Minsk II cease-fire. I am pleased to see you are looking at additional sanctions.

Understand that it is going to take U.S. leadership. If we wait for Europe to act, it is not going to be effective. We have to be out there with our European partners, but it is going to require U.S. leadership.

I want to change gears for one moment, if I might. I think we have had a lot of questioning on the defensive issues. I want to get to the economic front for one moment because my assessment from visiting Kyiv was that what happened in the protests there were as much about basic rights and economic rights as it was about political issues. So as we look to Ukraine being able to defend its borders and being able to control its territory, we also, at the same time, have to make sure that they have an effective government with the institutions that protect the rights of all of its citizens to express their views and to be treated fairly, free from corruption, as well as economic opportunities that that country should be able to provide for its citizens.

So I know the IMF originally made a commitment in 2014. I think it was $17 billion, $4.5 billion was released. They now have a new commitment that they entered into in February this year that looks like it takes this up to maybe $22 billion. I know the United States has provided some direct assistance.

But can you tell us how confident you are that the Ukrainian Government is moving toward the development of the institutions critical for democracy to flourish and how successful we are on their path for economic reform?

Mr. TOLOUI. Senator Cardin, thank you very much for that question.

I could not agree more that what we saw in the Maidan and what we have seen since reflects the desire of the Ukrainian people for a better life, including a better economic life. And I think that one reason that we have been successful in mobilizing such large international financial assistance for Ukraine is because the actions that the Ukrainian Government has taken reflect a decisive break from the past. Their willingness to address subsidies and inefficiencies and corruption in their government spending and their state-owned enterprises, establishing an anticorruption bureau, and addressing issues related to insider influence within financial institutions, all of these are actions that the Ukrainian Government has put forward, not that the international financial institutions have imposed on Ukraine. And when Secretary Lew or Under Secretary Nathan Sheets or myself have visited Ukraine in the last couple of months, the departure from the past practices of Ukrainian governments could not be more evident.

So our responsibility is to ensure that the international community, and the United States as part of the international community, is doing everything it can to support this reform agenda that the Ukrainian Government has embraced and has been embraced by huge legislative majorities in the recently elected Ukrainian parliament.

Senator CARDIN. Is there more that the United States should be doing? Are we satisfied with the IMF package? Are other countries coming forward with appropriate aid also?

Mr. TOLOUI. We think that we have the right package right now. We are satisfied with the IMF package. As you know, the United States had provided a $1 billion loan guarantee for Ukraine last year. We intend to provide another one in the first half of this year and are working with Congress to consider another $1 billion loan guarantee at the end of this year. So we appreciate congressional support for that.

In terms of other countries, we have had Europe and other bilateral donors increase their assistance to Ukraine in recent months. That is something that the senior officials within the Treasury, as well as the State Department, have worked on and we are going to continue to work on. We think that this government merits continued support not only from the United States but from other countries and international financial institutions.

Senator CARDIN. And I support the packages. I think we are doing the right thing.

But I just urge us—our support for Ukraine must include accountability and progress being made in regards to governance issues and human rights issues, and we have to make that very clear. We will be patient, but we will not have indefinite patience. They must demonstrate their ability to carry out their verbal commitments to their people, and we have to be tough about that.

I would ask one last question, if I might, and that is an assessment of the OSCE mission. As you know, one of the hats I wear is the ranking Democrat on the Helsinki Commission. Can someone give me an assessment as to how effective the OSCE has been in Ukraine?

Ms. NULAND. Senator, well, first, thank you for the work that you do with the OSCE. I think this is a tool of foreign policy and of European policy that was underutilized until the Ukraine crisis. Without the eyes and ears of the OSCE, I would not have been able to give the rundown that I gave of where things are going well and where things are going poorly in Ukraine at the beginning of this hearing.

That said, as you know, they are an unarmed force. They can only operate in a permissive environment. So that has been one of the challenges that they have had, whether it was getting into secure the crash site after Malaysian Air Line 17 or whether it has been now working, particularly in separatist-held areas, to get the kind of access that they need. So that is what we have to continue to work on.

We are trying to work now with European partners to make sure that every OSCE nation carries its weight in terms of fielding monitors, in terms of paying the budget increases that this requires, but also in terms of the specialized skills. We now need OSCE monitors who know the difference between an X kind of artillery piece and a Smerch rocket and that kind of thing. So we are working on all that.

Senator CARDIN. Thank you.

Thank you, Mr. Chairman.

The CHAIRMAN. Senator Isakson.

Senator ISAKSON. Thank you, Chairman Corker.

The chairman and I were in a private meeting this morning. So I cannot quote by name the individual but it is a very well respected journalist and commentator in America who was asked the question about what is the greatest threat to the United States security. Ironically, although acknowledging ISIL and obviously what we all know is going on in the Middle East, he directly cited the threat of Putin to disrupt NATO and destroy NATO as the biggest threat to the United States and the world, as he saw it, in the outlying years.

So, Secretary McKeon and Admiral Pandolfe, I would like your opinion on that statement.

Mr. McKEON. Senator Isakson, I would, in some respects, defer to the IC and its judgment of current threats to United States security. In terms of the terrorist threat, ISIL is certainly a threat. AQAP and core al-Qaeda is still a threat to the United States, as are other branches of al-Qaeda and ISIL.

We are certainly worried about the negative trend of Russia and what it is doing not just in Ukraine but along Europe's borders, and it is the core of the reason we have taken a lot of reassurance measures that we have and thinking hard about making sure that the alliance commitment can be met not just through the United States but through all of our NATO partners.

Senator ISAKSON. Admiral.

Admiral PANDOLFE. Senator, traditionally degree of threat is defined as capability and intent. In terms of capability, you know, the Russians are a world-class state with a world-class military. In terms of intent, that makes it even more important that we do the kinds of initiatives we have talked about this morning to try to shape the intent to minimize the risk.

Senator ISAKSON. Well, thank you for those answers.

You know, one good benefit of older age, which I am enjoying, is you have a long memory of experiences you went through in your life. One of the ones I went through is the Cuban missile crisis in the 1960s, and there are some—I am not drawing a total comparison, but some comparison to what Khrushchev did in trying to put missiles in Cuba and what Kennedy did in response and the potential of what is going on in the Ukraine because finally President Kennedy put a blockade around Cuba and called Khrushchev's bluff. And when he did, Khrushchev pulled his missiles out and went home.

I do not think we are at that place yet by any stretch of the imagination, but you all spend a lot of your careers looking into the future and saying ''what if.'' And so I think it is a lot of what Senator Johnson was saying. What if things get worse? We need to be prepared to be able to have the same type of response to match the threat with the force necessary to thwart that threat.

Am I right or wrong on that?

Mr. McKEON. Senator, in the Department of Defense, we are always worrying about the threats right in front of us but also the threats in the future, and we do a lot of planning to look out ahead. And the military modernization of Russia and its activities in central Europe have, no doubt, got the mind focus on looking ahead at various permutations of what Russia might do. So it is definitely an area of concern that we are giving a lot of thought and attention to in the Department.

Senator ISAKSON. Well, I know you have to be careful in your answer. And I will get to you, Admiral. And I respect that an understand that. But I think it is a fair enough comparison to underscore the needs. I think this committee feels in its entirety for us to look down at possible calculations down the line and be prepared to confront power with power and threat with threat.

Admiral.

Admiral PANDOLFE. I would just like to underline what Mr. McKeon said and to your point, Senator. I mean, readiness is absolutely key to deterrence. It is fundamental to what we do, and it is coupled to, as Assistant Secretary Nuland has said, Alliance solidarity. Those elements together are the best way to buy down risk and ensure stability and security.

Senator ISAKSON. Secretary Nuland, I want to ask you a question for my own edification. Would you consider Russia's use of its infinite supply of natural gas and oil soft power?

Ms. NULAND. Certainly its use of energy as a weapon. I do not know if I would call it soft, but it is certainly a tool of its influence.

Senator ISAKSON. My question—I do not know the answer to this. This is not a loaded question. It is one that is going to show my ignorance probably. But had their been a counterbalance to the supply of petroleum and gas that Russia could supply in that part of the world, could that have thwarted what Russia has done in the Ukraine and Crimea?

Ms. NULAND. Well, I think their interest in controlling supplies of energy to Europe is a factor. There were many other factors at play in Russia's decisions that it made in Ukraine.

Senator ISAKSON. But an alternative supply available to the Ukraine would have made possibly a difference in how far Russia went early on? And I am not trying to bait you. I am just trying to understand your——

Ms. NULAND. Yes. I mean, I think if Ukraine had been able to be more energy independent earlier in its period since independence from the Soviet Union, it would have had more resilience, and it would have had more ability to resist. And that is one of the reasons why we are putting so much effort now in the bilateral program into energy diversification, energy security for Ukraine, as well as for the rest of Europe.

Senator ISAKSON. And the reason I asked the question is it is important for us to understand the national defense interest of developing all the petroleum resources we can in the United States so we have control to kind of balance what the Russians are able to do in Russia.

Thank you all for your time and your interest.

The CHAIRMAN. Thank you.

Senator Kaine.

Senator KAINE. Thank you, Mr. Chairman, and thanks to the witnesses.

I want to pick up on where Senator Isakson left off, and then I have some questions about the economy and energy issues.

I have been a strong supporter of the economic sanctions against Russia, and I understand there have been earlier questions about the possibility of more sanctions in the energy sector. It does seem this is the economic tool that Russia uses most. So whether it is sanctions in the energy sector or helping nations that over-rely on Russia to have alternate sources of energy or to develop their own sources of energy, these are all strategies that I strongly support.

But Senator Johnson made a comment repeating some comments from a hearing last week, and I am just interested in your theories about it. To the extent that we are more successful in economic sanctions, to the extent that an extended period of low oil prices, for example, puts economic pressure on Russia, there was some testimony in the hearing last week that that makes Russia more dangerous militarily. And I would be curious as to your thoughts on that. I am a supporter of sanctions and energy pressure, but does that raise the risk of unpredictable military behavior?

Mr. MCKEON. Senator Kaine, I do not know that it raises the risks or makes Russia more dangerous. It is hard to understate the provocations and dangers of the actions President Putin has already taken. He is going to face some hard economic choices if oil prices stay down and capital flight continues and the ruble continues in the direction it is going. He has got a big investment in his military modernization. It is a big part of his budget. And as I say, if the oil prices stay down, he is going to have to make some hard choices. If he continues to sustain those investments, there are going to be some other costs I suspect in the social safety net in Russia. So he is going to have to weigh that in terms of his internal politics. I know it is not exactly a democracy, but he does have to pay attention to what is going on in the country and public attitudes.

Senator KAINE. Any different positions?

[No response.]

Senator KAINE. So this is not something we should be overly concerned about if we decide to do more sanctions in the energy sector or take steps to help Ukraine and other nations diversify their energy portfolio?

Then let me follow up and ask about this issue of the internal Russian dynamic. There has been a lot of question of how much are the sanctions having an effect, how much are low oil prices having an effect. Clearly we have seen statistics about capital outflow, reduction in foreign direct investment, devaluation of the ruble, other economic effects. What is the best that you can tell me now in an unclassified setting about the combined effects of either sanctions or oil prices on the internal political dynamic in Russia today?

Ms. NULAND. Well, I think Assistant Secretary Toloui has given you some of the facts and figures that this policy has wrought, not only Russia's vulnerability to low oil prices because of their lack of economic diversification over the last 15 years, but also as a result of sanctions. I think we have yet to see what the political impacts will be, but we clearly can see from some of the statistics that Russian kitchen tables are being hit now by these policy choices that the Kremlin are making. When you hear Assistant Secretary Toloui talk about inflation at 15 to 17 percent, when we have statistics of skyrocketing food prices across the Russian space, 20 to 40 percent in some places, when we know that average Russians are having difficulty paying for loans for apartments, for cars, when we see imports way down, it is affecting lifestyles. Now, that simply goes to the point that the Kremlin has prioritized their international adventure over the quality of life for their own people, and at what point that has a political effect, I think we have yet to see.

Senator KAINE. The question about where will oil prices be in a year is something of which we should be wary with respect to speculating, but there are people who have to make that speculation. Folks who buy fuel for major airlines, et cetera have to do projections all the time, and some of their projections are that oil prices would stay in this low range for some extended period of time.

If we are a year from now and oil prices have stayed in basically this historically low level, talk a little bit about what you would predict that you would see in terms of the internal Russian economic dynamic, and then we can draw the line between that and likely political feelings.

Mr. TOLOUI. Senator Kaine, thank you for that.

I think it is important to recognize that the economic outcomes that we have seen in Russia have really been an interaction between what we have seen in oil and the impact of economic sanctions. Higher oil prices would definitely be a positive for the Russian economy.

But I think it is relevant to look at what both Moody's and S&P have done to Russia's credit rating. Russia has been downgraded to junk for the first time since 2003–2004. Now, the responsibility of agencies like Moody's and S&P is not to react to what the oil price is today but to think about how Russia's economy is being managed, what the impact of sanctions is, and how that affects the Russian Government's ability to meet its obligations not only to foreign creditors but to its people.

And so I think that if we saw higher oil prices—and I am not going to speculate on oil prices like you mentioned. But I think that even if we see oil prices rise, the combination of economic mismanagement and the impact of sanctions has cast the shadow on Russian economic prospects that is expected to persist. And one manifestation of that is the decision of the rating agencies to designate Russian debt as junk.

Senator KAINE. Thank you, Mr. Chair. I do not have other questions.

The CHAIRMAN. Senator Rubio.

Senator RUBIO. Thank you. Thank you all for being here.

Secretary Nuland, in your statement, you outline our goal as threefold. First, we want peace, then political normalization, and then ultimately the return to borders, which I imagine includes Crimea as well. The question that I have is how realistic—and the hope is that Minsk would offer that promise with peace coming first as the precondition for all these things to be possible.

The question that I have is how realistic is that goal, given the goals that Putin has himself. I think the goal, unless any of you dispute this—I think the goal Putin has here is to basically—it is not just about Ukraine. It is about completely reorganizing the post-cold-war, post-Soviet-era order in Europe. And it is not just about Ukraine.

And in that context, that is why he wants to weaken and divide and perhaps even force NATO to fall apart. In fact, he has questioned why we even need a NATO anymore since there is no more Soviet Union. As part of furthering that goal, he has openly said that they believe they need to establish a sphere of influence and not just throughout the former Soviet space but also in former Warsaw Pact type countries.

This whole talk about protecting Russian speakers—this is just an excuse that he puts out there as a justification before the international community for moving forward. But ultimately their goal, their ultimate goal, here is to carve out, to reorder the post-Soviet order in the region and to carve out for Russia a strategic space, for themselves, of influence.

And so in light of that, why should we have any hope that these cease-fires are actually going to hold, given we know what his ultimate goal is? Now, he may agree to a temporary cease-fire as a tactical move maybe hopefully to split us off from the Europeans, in essence hoping for us to act. And maybe that is why there have been arguments that we should not go on sanctions alone because it could cause friction with the European Union and split us from them in that regard. But at the end of the day, he may agree to a cease-fire temporarily either to consolidate gains they have already made or to perhaps try to create a point of friction between—hoping that we will jump out ahead of the Europeans and create that as a division. But ultimately his goal unquestionably is to completely rearrange the order in this area and carve out for Russia a sphere of influence.

So how is it even realistic, knowing that about him, to think that he is ever going to allow stabilization to return to Ukraine and that he is ever going to return back to their borders, given we know what their goal is. I mean, he is a criminal and a thug, but he is also a very determined one who has shown the willingness to act out in furtherance of a strategic goal. So why should I feel optimistic that there is any chance of that happening, given the goal he has now, unless the cost/benefit analysis changes for him?

Ms. NULAND. Senator, I am not going to dispute any of your analysis. I am simply going to say that Minsk is a test for Russia. Russia signed it. The separatists signed it. It is also a choice for Russia. If fully implemented, it would bring back sovereignty and territorial integrity in the east. It does not, obviously, address Crimea.

So now we have to test. And as I said at the beginning, the record is already mixed today, and we have to be ready both for the opportunity for success but also to impose more costs, significant costs, on Russia, with our European partners, if Minsk is violated either because the agreement is not implemented or because there is a further land grab or because the separatists are further armed. And that is what we are watching.

Senator RUBIO. So in furtherance of that question, if in fact this is a test, what is wrong with now laying out clearly exactly what we are going to do if that test has failed. In essence, if this test fails, we are going to arm the Ukrainians with—by the way, as a sovereign country, Ukraine has a right to defend itself not just against Russian aggression or separatist aggression but any aggression. If in fact we are trying to strengthen the writ of that government, part of that is allowing them to provide for their own defense. So we should be doing that anyway.

But is it the position of the administration that we are going to lay out a clear picture, hopefully with your European partners, of what the specific sanctions will be and what specific military aid we will provide if Russia fails the Minsk test?

Ms. NULAND. Senator, I think in my opening I made clear that we are working now with the Europeans to lay out concrete sanctions costs if Minsk is not implemented or further violated. We generally do not signal those in advance, but we make it clear that we are prepared, and that is what we are working on. With regard to security assistance, we are continuing to evaluate that based on the situation on the ground, and implementation of Minsk will very much be part of that.

Senator RUBIO. Can you comment on whether denying Russia access to the SWIFT system is something that has been discussed?

Mr. TOLOUI. We actually generally do not discuss in a public forum any specific measures, but we discuss a whole range of things. As we are evaluating it, we look at both the impact that it would have on Russia, as well as the spillovers that it would have on the global economy, the United States, and our European partners. But I do not want to comment on any specific action.

Senator RUBIO. My last question, I guess, is just more of a— maybe I do not expect you to comment on this. But irrespective of whether Russia adheres to Minsk or not, if in fact we want to stabilize Ukraine, is not part of that stabilization to give them the ability to defend themselves in the future from any other aggression that may exist? In essence, there are other countries that have not been invaded who we provide military assistance to and defensive systems to because we understand that the absence of it invites aggression in the future. I just want to know why is it a bad idea to provide them defensive systems irrespective—and I know that is being reviewed. But is there an argument to be made against providing defensive weapons to a country irrespective of how the cease-fire turns out since we are trying to help them stabilize their government and as part of that, it has to be the ability to provide for their national defense?

Mr. MCKEON. Senator Rubio, as you know, we have provided a range of security assistance in the nonlethal categories which have met real Ukrainian security requirements because the armed forces were not fully stripped bare, but they were left rather lacking by the corruption of the last regime. And I expect long past this crisis, we will have a defense partnership with the Government of Ukraine, but at the present time, as Assistant Secretary Nuland said, defensive lethal weapons are being reviewed but it is not something on offer at the present time.

Senator RUBIO. And my last question is—I have heard some commentary that even among Putin's critics within Russia there are those who do not support giving defensive weapons to Ukraine because ultimately that would lead to the death of Russians, and they cannot support that. I read that yesterday. I think The Washington Post reported or had some commentary from some of Putin's opponents.

So here is my question. If Putin says there are no Russian troops in Ukraine, therefore, if we provided—if that is true, he has nothing to worry about. Right?

Ms. NULAND. As I made clear in my opening, not only do we believe that there are Russian forces in Ukraine, we believe that they are responsible for command and control, arming, financing, directing of this conflict. We also believe that there are many hundreds of Russians dead in Ukraine and that it does pose a vulnerability for the Kremlin politically at home because they are denying they are even active there.

Senator RUBIO. Sorry. Just one quick point. I read in your statement—maybe you did not say this publicly because you had to shorten your statement. Is it not accurate that as these coffins are returning and these bodies are returning to Russia, Russian families of the dead soldiers are being told not to comment on it or they will be denied death benefits?

Ms. NULAND. Yes, and I did say that publicly here.

Senator RUBIO. Thank you.

The CHAIRMAN. Thank you.

I know Senator Menendez had a closing question for this panel.

Senator MENENDEZ. Well, thank you, Mr. Chairman, and thank you all for your testimony.

Madam Secretary, the Budapest Memorandum was basically a way to entice the Ukrainians to give up their nuclear weapons. Is that a fair statement?

Ms. NULAND. Ranking Member Menendez, at the time the primary intent was to get Russia to assure Ukraine that it would not seek to take advantage of Ukraine's sovereignty and territorial integrity if it gave up its weapons. So Ukraine sought that political guarantee primarily from Russia, and it is that guarantee that Russia has violated. There was never an intent to have treaty obligations——

Senator MENENDEZ. No. I gather that from your answer to Senator Murphy. You said it was a political agreement. Right? Yes?

Ms. NULAND. Yes.

Senator MENENDEZ. All right. So we also, however, signed that political agreement, and so while you say the concern for Ukraine was Russia not seeking to attack it or to interfere with its territorial integrity if it did what? If it gave up its nuclear weapons. Right? That is the essence of what was induced from the Ukrainians. Is that not fair to say? Whether it was that they wanted a guarantee from Russia and we just joined with Great Britain and others to sort of like give them further comfort in this political agreement, it was to give up their nuclear arms because otherwise there is no reason for such an agreement.

Ms. NULAND. Senator, they also sought assurance from the other two nuclear powers, the United States and Great Britain, that we would not seek to exploit Ukrainian sovereignty and territorial integrity. And we obviously have not done that. So that was the structure of the agreement.

Senator MENENDEZ. But the whole purpose of it was to guarantee territorial integrity and not to face the threat from any of these powers if it did what? Give up its nuclear weapons. Is that correct?

Ms. NULAND. Of course.

Senator MENENDEZ. I do not know why we are dancing around.

Ms. NULAND. No. Of course.

Senator MENENDEZ. It is about giving up their nuclear weapons.

Ms. NULAND. Of course, and they did that.

Senator MENENDEZ. So how is this political agreement different than the one we are trying to strike with Iran? Is basically the agreement we are trying to strike with Iran not a political agreement because it is not a treaty obligation the administration has said?

Ms. NULAND. I am not, as you know, qualified to get into the intricacies of the deal that we are trying to strike with Iran. I think I will leave that to the folks in the administration who work on Iran.

Senator MENENDEZ. I am not asking you about the intricacies of the agreement. That is for another time with another panel.

The question is it seems to me that what we have heard from the administration, as it relates to Iran, is to say that it is not going to be a treaty, therefore the Congress has no need to have a say. It is going to be basically a political agreement. And if that is the case, then we need to know the nature of what that means. As I see it unfolding here in the Budapest Memorandum, which was a political agreement ultimately to entice the Ukrainians to give up their nuclear weapons, which they did with an understanding that all of these powers were not going to affect its territorial integrity, which in the case of Russia has been violated. So I do not see the difference, and I do think it is very much on point.

So it raises concerns for me as to where we are going in that regard. But you tell me you are not capable of answering that question.

Ms. NULAND. Well, let me just say that with regard to the Budapest political commitment, the United States of America lived up to its commitments under Budapest. So if the concern is whether the United States honors political commitments as it honors treaties, I think one can be reassured by our behavior vis-a-vis Budapest. I cannot speak to other nations.

Senator MENENDEZ. We have certainly, nor did we ever have any intention of interfering with Ukraine's territorial integrity. The reason that we joined is to give comfort, support, and I think the Ukrainians would think that in fact that political agreement with these three powers—because I doubt that the Ukrainians ever thought that we were going to somehow invade their territory—was in fact that we would be supportive of their security and their territorial integrity. But at this point, while we certainly have not done anything to interfere with its integrity, I think the Ukrainians would feel far short of what that agreement meant in terms of its actual implementation. And so at the end of the day, it is a political agreement that can be interpreted as those who signed it wish to interpret it. And that is, I think, a challenging proposition.

The CHAIRMAN. I very much appreciate the line of questioning the ranking member just put forth.

I have to say this has been a very good hearing. We thank all of you for your testimony.

It has been very unsatisfying to me. I would ask the Secretary who does meet with people constantly around the world. Surely on the heels of us never doing the things we said we would do with the Free Syrian Army rebels and now the world being very aware of this Budapest Memorandum and knowing that this is another decision memo that sits on the President's desk undecided.

This has to have affected our credibility with others around the world. I would love to have your sense of that and how damaging our lack of ability make simple decisions—they certainly have complex outcomes, but the decisions themselves are relatively simple, certainly highly supported by Congress. So we are all in this together should a decision be made.

But I would just like to get your sense of how badly, on the heels again of what we never did in Syria, on the heels of a redline that was never adhered to, and this particular issue which is so important to world stability—I would love to get your sense of how this is affecting us with others.

Ms. NULAND. Well, Chairman, I would say with regard to my patch, Europeans do see these strong bipartisan, bicameral support for Ukraine, whether it is on the economic side or on the security side—and frankly per capita, we have done—well, I do not want to say "per capita," but we have done far more than most nations in the transatlantic space to support Ukraine. And I do think that our leadership in this is recognized. As spirited a debate as is ongoing inside the administration on some of these security support questions, there is also a transatlantic debate. So that question gets asked also in our diplomacy. But the Europeans come at it from both sides depending upon where they sit.

The CHAIRMAN. Well, we are going to have the record open for questions and move into a second panel.

I would just say that I have very much enjoyed our conversations. You have been very forward with your statements regarding Ukraine and the things that need to be done, and that has been appreciated very much by most of us.

I would have, at this point, significant difficulty coming to work each day with these decisions lingering in the way that they have and us, again, not taking the steps that many people within the administration, as I understand it, feel need to be taken. And yet, we continue for some reason not to do those things that we have acted as if we might do.

So I have a number of other questions that I will send in writing, and I thank each of you for being here. I realize that in all cases you all are messengers and not the ones that have these decision memos sitting on your desk unheralded. But we thank you for your service to our country and appreciate your candid testimony.

With that, we will move to the second panel.

Our first witness is former Assistant Secretary of State for European Affairs and former U.S. Ambassador to Germany, John Kornblum. Our second and final witness on this panel is former U.S. Ambassador to Ukraine and Director of the Eurasia Center at The Atlantic Council, John Herbst.

And as you all are getting seated and comfortable, we will begin with Ambassador Kornblum.

Ambassador Kornblum, I do want to thank you for being here in particular. I know you are a resident of Nashville, TN, and we are always glad to have really bright people from Nashville, TN, here testifying. With that, if you would begin, we would appreciate it.

## STATEMENT OF HON. JOHN C. KORNBLUM, FORMER ASSISTANT SECRETARY OF STATE FOR EUROPEAN AFFAIRS, AND FORMER UNITED STATES AMBASSADOR TO GERMANY, BERLIN, GERMANY

Ambassador KORNBLUM. Thank you very much. You might even be more pleased to learn I have very direct contact with another city you know, Chattanooga, TN. And Mr. Mayor Berke is going to be at a meeting that I am organizing in Berlin in 3 weeks to talk about the tremendous success that Chattanooga has had in revitalizing the city and supporting entrepreneurship there. And I think you had a little bit to do with that. I have heard that anyway from history.

And so I am very pleased to be here both because of my ties to Tennessee and also because these are issues that I worked upon a lot in the 1990s. I was the Assistant Secretary during this whole period involved in all these memorandum and these agreements and participated in the negotiation of most of them, not the Budapest paper but most of the others. And so to you and also to Ranking Member Menendez, I am very pleased to be here.

I have a very special point to make. You have heard in extremely good detail if not always satisfying detail about how our Government sees things. But I think there is one thing that we need to think about which Senator Rubio in particular talked about, and that is the direction of this conflict and the definition of this conflict.

My own view is—and I have been living in Germany for a long time now after I stopped being Ambassador. And I think that I can say with a certain amount of accuracy that whatever we are doing in Ukraine and with Russia, we are losing the public affairs battle on this crisis, the narrative as we say in the journalistic world.

The narrative that is most prevalent, in the United States to a considerable extent but more so even in Europe, is that this is a Russia which is reacting angrily because it was cheated, ill-used, misused by the West after 1990. And I think it is important that we focus on this fact because many of the decisions—and let me say a couple points about that—which are going to be taken in the future will depend considerably on whether the Russians believe that they have the upper hand on this aspect of the crisis and whether we, in fact, can maintain a strong situation and a strong direction.

The fact is that after 1990, we dealt with the Russian leadership which saw the collapse of the Soviet Union as a liberation and not as a Western attack on Russia. And they knew exactly what our plans were. We talked to them in great detail about it. We did not talk to them about the details of NATO enlargement or EU enlargement, but we certainly told them that our goal for them and for Europe was to establish democracy, establish free market systems, and to allow Russia to join the Western world. And on many of the discussions I had, Ambassador Herbst was along, and I think he can attest to this. We worked very hard to make this point not only clear but to establish things to make it real.

And now, 20–25 years later, for me the narrative of this crisis is not whether Russia somehow is now a wounded power, but the fact that the United States, three administrations in connection also working with the Congress, have established between the Baltic States and now, hopefully, Ukraine also, and the south, a community of nearly a billion persons, which is democratic, which is secure, which is oriented toward free markets, and which wants to be part of the Western and the Atlantic world.

Now, I say this so precisely because we have to remember what the situation was 25 years ago. Twenty-five years ago, we had the western part of the continent democratized. The eastern part was, to put it mildly, a mess. When we first came in to establish relations with the new governments in Poland and Czechoslovakia, Hungary, we found that they had hardly any of the basic conditions for modern industrial Western society. And so the cooperation within NATO, with the strong leadership of these countries, has in fact succeeded.

And many of the reasons that we have this conflict with Russia right now is not because Ukraine violated orders or not because Russia has somehow felt threatened by the West. It is because the leadership in Russia, after the beginning of this century, has covered its own misdeeds, its own poor performance with an increase in the authoritarian system, and they are finding that the countries on their periphery, but also until recently, much of their population wanted to join the West and not to maintain an eastern orientation.

This is the basic point, and it leads to strategy, however. It suggests, for example, that entering into negotiations with the Russians over how to conclude this crisis are not very relevant at the moment. There is not any new security system which we can offer the Russians which would not include giving them a sphere of influence in these very countries we are trying to protect. There is not any military arrangement which we can enter with the Russians which would not somehow limit our ability to defend these countries to the east who we have helped become democratic. There is not any new political forum which we can think up which would change the fact that the real reason that Putin and his cohorts in Russia in general feel threatened at the moment. It is not because of anything we have done and not because of NATO sanctions even, although I favor them, but because of things such as—it has all been discussed here today—the oil price, Russia's lack of investment in the high-tech sector, Russia's inability to build the infra-structure necessary for a modern industrial economy, et cetera, et cetera.

It also, I think, has to do with the fact that Russia—Mr. Herbst is more of an expert on this than I am—has, in fact, also failed to have the political leadership since 2000 which helped its population come out of the shock of the end of the cold war and to understand how closely its interests are involved with being part of the West.

So we have a situation now which is important for all the reasons that our Government officials mentioned to you today. They gave, I thought, a very comprehensive view of what is going on. But we are, in effect, facing an even larger challenge, a challenge which is not only a challenge to Europe but a challenge actually across the entire world, and that is that Russia, whether consciously or by accident, is taking account of a growing unease around the world at the dislocations caused by what is called ''globalization,'' what is the modern information technology world, what is happening with the dislocation of industries, et cetera, et cetera, and that the Russians have been able to harness this dissatisfaction in their own country.

But I can tell you with, shall I say, a lot of experience—I have been living in Berlin now for 17 years and I am still very politically active there—that these arguments are also having an effect in Western Europe, and they are also having an effect, as you know, in other parts of the world.

Add to that—one of the Senators mentioned it—Russia is financing, with very large efforts, movements in Western Europe who are antidemocratic, who are trying to undermine the Western system. And Russia is also continuing to threaten in one way or the other the weakest points of our system such as the Baltic States, such as the Republic of Georgia, where I worked quite diligently in recent years. And so we are facing not just the question—and it is a very important question.

I might add that I will mention to Senator Murphy that my wife grew up in the Ukrainian community in Hartford, CT. And so she is very oriented toward Ukraine, has been an election observer there twice already. So we are very committed to Ukraine.

But the real challenge of this crisis is that Russia, after immense efforts on the part of the West—and I must say really immense efforts—has broken out of the channel of unity and cooperation among the countries of Europe and is now adapting an anti-Western—but ultimately that means anti-globalization and anti-American approach.

And to understand the importance of this, there was an extremely good article in The Washington Post this week talking about the rhetoric that is being used inside China about the West. And it turns out to be almost word for word the same rhetoric that Russia is using. The same rhetoric is heard in the Middle East. And even in India, which we consider to be a very important partner, Putin has been visiting, and the Indian leadership more or less agreed with many of the things he was saying.

So we are talking here not just about a problem with Russia, which is an important one. We are talking, in fact—and that is why I mentioned Senator Rubio—about a wearing away at the foundations of the Western community in Europe but, even more so, a wearing away of the ability that the West is going to have to influence, control if you will, the content of the new globalized world which is coming up. And so that is the main consequence that I see in this conflict.

And my final point would be I am very appreciative of your personal efforts to increase our information budgets, to have Radio Liberty and Radio Free Europe be more active. And I think that winning back the narrative and using tools such as the ones that you are financing is almost as important as considering military support for Ukraine, which I support very strongly.

Thank you.

[The prepared statement of Ambassador Kornblum follows:]

### PREPARED STATEMENT OF JOHN C. KORNBLUM

Senator Corker, members of the committee, I am honored to have been invited to join your hearing on the crisis in Ukraine. I was a frequent guest of this committee and its members during the 1990s in my role as Assistant Secretary of State and Special Envoy to the Balkans. I look forward to our discussion of ways in which Russian strategy can be countered.

In those years, we cooperated to establish conditions for a peaceful, democratic transition for nations of the former Warsaw Pact. Congressional support for economic and humanitarian aid to Russia, the economic support funds extended to Eastern Europe and the tireless efforts of Senators Nunn, Lugar, and many others to reduce the threat of nuclear weapons in the former Soviet Union, including in Ukraine, were essential to our success.

In the London Summit Declaration of July 6, 1990, NATO promised to "reach out to the countries of the East which were our adversaries in the cold war and extend to them the hand of friendship." The London document also presented ideas for an important strengthening of the OSCE, which were agreed at the Helsinki summit 2 years later.

First assessments of conditions in the former Warsaw Pact in 1990 were pessimistic to say the least. These countries had been stripped of their talent and identity and left with few of the structures of modern political or economic life.

But Western assistance and the dedication of their own peoples worked a near miracle. One by one the nations of Central Europe departed intensive care. Today, we can be proud of the secure and prosperous democratic community of nearly 1 billion inhabitants which stretches from the east of Europe to the tip of Alaska.

Membership of both NATO and the European Union gave these countries the stability and the technical assistance necessary to succeed. It was in no way aimed at isolating Russia.

Many of the Russian leaders with whom we dealt in those years welcomed these efforts. They viewed the collapse of the Soviet Union as liberation rather than defeat. They embraced hopes for Western democracy as the best path to both security and freedom for their country.

I repeat this history, because it so contradicts the version of post-cold-war events we now often hear. Today it is our economic and political success which threatens Russia's authoritarians rulers, not our soldiers. Those who find logic in Russian criticism of Western behavior 20 years ago have perhaps not asked residents of Estonia or Slovakia how they feel about NATO expansion.

This is why the Russian counterattack, military and digital, has been so vicious. Current Russia leaders appear to view the growing encroachment of the Western way of life as an existential challenge.

I am one who favors military assistance to help Ukraine regain its footing. But I believe that a substantially expanded public presentation of the facts could be equally as important.

Why? Because at the moment, Putin's ability to control public perceptions is severely hindering efforts to stop the fighting and restore order in Ukraine. And, for the moment at least, the West is losing the rhetorical battle.

Russia has invested immense resources into applying the tools of globalization to a massive program of disinformation. It has combined nationalism within Russia, with the legend of a proud nation humbled by the evil West and added an extra dose of old fashioned anti-Americanism to shoot an unbroken stream of invective around the world.

Putin is also using the same methods to influence the self-styled Western ''realists'' who seem not to understand that Russia's anger has little to do with NATO or European security structures. Bowing to Putin's imperial pretensions will do nothing to redress the falling oil price, Russia's failure to invest in new technology or the flow of talented scientists and technicians to the West.

In other words, the Russian attack on Ukraine has already expanded into what is probably the world's first digitally managed diplomatic confrontation. Normal people, rich and poor are increasingly worried that they are losing control of their destinies to something called globalization. Putin has been able to harness these fears in a desperate effort to return the narrative to issues of the past.

He wants us to believe that the crisis is really about the way in which the West suppresses countries like Russia which don't follow the American lead. However far-fetched it may seem, this image of Western betrayal is attractive to many non-European and even some European countries who also feel put upon by the West. The echo has helped Putin justify his unbroken flow of troops and materiel into Ukraine. At the same time, Russian aggression has provided Ukraine one thing which was so far lacking—national purpose.

Unless the United States and its allies wrest the rhetorical high ground from Russia, Mr. Putin is likely to become more arrogant and thus more dangerous. His sense of media control could ultimately make him overconfident and prone to disastrous mistakes. Senator Corker I congratulate you for your efforts to strengthen our information activities in the region.

Championing the need to ensure a democratic operating system for digital society is today the equivalent of our support for political democracy during the cold war. The radical integration of the world through high speed information networks and modern logistics is redrawing the global geostrategic map before our very eyes.

Everyone, including Russia, will profit if we ensure that the principles of Western democracy are firmly established as the basis for global integration. If, however, we allow the debate to lend credence to those who reject the openness of Western values, it won't stop at Russia or Ukraine, or even in Europe. China is already mounting a counterattack. We could see the digital world rapidly deconstructing into competing cultural fiefdoms.

Above all this crisis demonstrates that in a networked world, there are no longer any unimportant far away countries. Every place on earth can become central to our concerns if the factors line up correctly. One of the main jobs of a new generation of digital diplomats will be to learn how to judge the factors which influence such network behavior better than we have done so far.

The CHAIRMAN. Thank you.
Ambassador.

## STATEMENT OF HON. JOHN HERBST, FORMER UNITED STATES AMBASSADOR TO UKRAINE; DIRECTOR, DINU PATRICIU EURASIA CENTER, THE ATLANTIC COUNCIL, WASHINGTON, DC

Ambassador HERBST. Chairman Corker, Ranking Member Menendez, thank you very much for this chance to testify. It is an honor to be here.

I have been asked to talk about Kremlin aggression in Ukraine and how to counter it. But in order to take this subject on properly, we need a wider lens. The reason for this is simple. There are influential people in the United States and especially in Europe who do not understand the gravity of this crisis. They do not understand it because they think the crisis is simply about Ukraine and Moscow's aggression there. With that narrow understanding, they oppose the strong measures necessary to counter Kremlin aggression and to secure vital—and I mean vital—American interests, not simply important interests.

The crisis that we face is, as I think almost every Senator today said, a crisis of Kremlin revisionism. Mr. Putin does want to overturn the post-cold-war order established in Europe and Eurasia. This order has been the foundation of the unprecedented peace and prosperity that not just Europe but the entire world has enjoyed over the past 25 years. Mr. Putin has stated that he must have a sphere of influence in the post-Soviet space, not just the post-Russian world; his concerns extend into the Warsaw Pact countries and he has the right to protect ethnic Russians and Russian speakers wherever they reside.

Mr. Putin has major resources to pursue aggression. He possesses the world's sixth-largest economy, one of the world's two largest nuclear arsenals, and far and away the strongest military in Europe.

And we all know Mr. Putin has committed multiple acts of aggression in Georgia in 2008, in Crimea early last year, and since April of last year, he has been conducting an increasingly overt, covert war in Ukraine's east.

In this covert war in Ukraine's east, he has escalated his intervention multiple times. He has agreed to two cease-fires, Minsk I and Minsk II, and violated each one of them. His goal in Ukraine is what the Admiral said earlier today, to destabilize the country. But to achieve that—and this is not clearly understood—he cannot settle for a frozen conflict. He needs to be regularly on the offensive, albeit with tactical pauses.

He has made clear by his statements and his actions that if he succeeds in Ukraine, there will be future targets. The targets may include NATO allies, specifically Estonia and Latvia, where ethnic Russians and Russia speakers comprise 25 percent of the population.

Recent Kremlin provocations include the kidnapping of an Estonia intelligence official from Estonia. And that happened on the day that the NATO summit ended last September. They have also included the seizure of a Lithuanian ship from international waters of the Baltic Sea. He is telling the Baltic States and all the states in his neighborhood that they are not secure even as members of NATO.

We have a vital interest—again I use that word ''vital''—in stopping Moscow's revanchist policies before they move to other countries, especially to the Baltic States.

I think it was Senator Isakson who said that the Kremlin menace is the most important national security danger we face today. I endorse that wholeheartedly. ISIL is a ragtag bunch of terrorists, a serious danger to individual Americans, not an existential threat to the United States. A revanchist Moscow is an existential threat to the United States. Even Iran with its nuclear program is not the same order of threat as Mr. Putin's Russia, one of the world's two largest nuclear powers and on the prowl. If Western leaders clearly understood this danger, they would devote substantially more resources to deal with it and they would draw a bright redline in Ukraine, stop Putin in Ukraine before he moves elsewhere.

To date, Western policy has been slow, reactive, and all too concerned about giving Mr. Putin a graceful way out of the crisis—and not sufficiently focused on imposing costs that would make it too expensive for him to continue his aggression. We had a very distinguished panel in the first 2 hours of this session, but they were all too reflective of a slow, reactive approach.

To persuade Mr. Putin to put aside his revisionist dreams, we need to do things that play on his weaknesses. Strong sanctions are part of this. We have to deal with Mr. Putin's economy. We must persuade Mr. Putin by announcing the strong additional sanctions for aggression to come. I think it was Senator Rubio who asked why we cannot tell Mr. Putin now what sanctions we will impose if he moves beyond the current cease-fire line. He asked a very good question. We need to have sanctions in place now if he moves again. Such proactive measures may deter aggression; but if he moves, they will impose costs for the aggression by weakening his economy, weakening his political support at home, and depriving him of resources for his next aggression. I give the Obama administration pretty good marks for dealing with sanctions because they are trying to pull along a somewhat reluctant Europe.

The other area we need to work on is on the security side. Mr. Putin has a serious vulnerability. The Russian people do not want Russian troops fighting in Ukraine. That is why he is lying to them. That is why the Russian dead that come back are buried in secret. That is why the families of the Russian dead are told that if they tell the neighbors that their sons fought and died in Ukraine, they will not get death benefits from the government.

If we provide defensive lethal equipment to Ukraine, that means that either Mr. Putin will be deterred from going further into Ukraine because he does not want to risk the casualties, and the political fallout of the casualties; or if he goes further into Ukraine, he suffers those casualties, and his support at home will weaken. This is a compelling reason to give weapons to Ukraine.

Some people who argue against supplying weapons say that if we do that, Mr. Putin will simply escalate. Perhaps. But if he escalates, again he suffers more casualties, he weakens his support, and he has fewer resources with which to pursue aggression beyond Ukraine.

I was one of a group of eight former officials who produced a report on this. We suggest giving Ukraine $1 billion a year for each of the next 3 years, $3 billion of weapons total. The report provides the details. I want to mention to this committee just two elements of that.

One, we should be providing antiarmor equipment because the Russians have used mass tanks in order to commit their aggression in Ukraine. We should also be providing counterbattery radar for missiles because Ukrainians have suffered 70 percent of their casualties from Russian missiles. We are giving them counterbattery radar for mortars. They need it for missiles.

We also need to keep in place the sanctions for the seizure of Crimea. And I should add the Atlantic Council just released a report on substantial systematic Russian human rights violations in Crimea.

I would like to briefly mention two other essential elements of our policy. We need to do more in NATO to bolster the deterrence to Russian aggression against the Baltic States. The administration and NATO have taken some good steps forward. The Wales summit talked about creating this rapid reaction force and deploying a company of soldiers to the Baltic States. That is a nice first step but it is very small. We should put a battalion into Estonia and the other Baltic States, properly armed as a serious trip wire against further Russian aggression. We need to make sure that NATO has a contingency plan dealing for a possible Russia hybrid war in the Baltic States. Especially vulnerable is Narva in Estonia, which is a Russian-speaking enclave.

Finally, we need to do the right thing in the information war against Russia. John already mentioned that. I know that this committee supports additional funding for Radio Free Europe and Radio Liberty. This is important to offsetting the massive Russian propaganda campaign.

These four steps, enhanced sanctions, military supplies to Ukraine, a much stronger military posture in NATO's east, and a ramped-up information effort, will give us a good, good start in stopping Mr. Putin in Ukraine, making sure he does not go beyond Ukraine. Again, this is a vital American interest.

[The prepared statement of Ambassador Herbst follows:]

PREPARED STATEMENT OF JOHN E. HERBST

Chairman Corker, Ranking Member Menendez, members of the committee, thank you for the invitation to speak this morning. It is an honor.

I have been asked to speak about the Kremlin's aggression in Ukraine and how the United States should counter this. In order to take on this subject properly, we need a wider focus. I will try to provide that wider focus here.

Over 1 year has passed since Moscow began its invasion of Ukraine, introducing to the world a new term: "little green men." Using these troops over 11 months ago, the Kremlin began its hybrid war in Ukraine's east. The political class in Washington, policymakers, and influence wielders are slowly coming to understand what is going on. In the most powerful capitals in Europe, the process is even slower. Only in the eastern reaches of Europe—Poland, the Baltic States, Romania, Moldova, Georgia—is the crisis in Ukraine properly understood. That is no surprise. Proper understanding of the crisis and an adequate response is essential for the very survival of these states.

Ukraine, the states of the former Soviet Union, NATO, and the EU face the problem of Kremlin revisionism. President Putin has stated on numerous occasions his dissatisfaction with the peace in Europe and Eurasia established at the end of the cold war. He has at his disposal substantial means for acting on his dissatisfaction and most important of all, he has used those means. It is time policymakers in major capitals understood this.

THE POST-COLD-WAR ORDER

What is the post-cold-war order that Mr. Putin finds so objectionable? It is the peace that emerged just before and after the dissolution of the Soviet Union with the following traits:

- The countries that were subservient to Moscow in the Warsaw Pact pursued independent internal and foreign policies;
- Due to an agreement accepted by the leaders of Russia, Ukraine, Belarus, and Kazakhstan, the Soviet Union dissolved and its constituent republics became independent states. (It is important to note that this decision was taken exclusively by Russian and other leaders in the Soviet Union. The West played no part in this and then President George H.W. Bush even advised against it.);
- It was understood that disputes in Europe would be resolved only by negotiations and other peaceful means;
- The tensions and geopolitical competition that characterized 20th century Europe and made it history's bloodiest were a thing of the past;
- To reduce political tensions and to promote prosperity, European integration would continue, including the countries of the former Soviet bloc; and
- Russia and the West were now partners, and ever closer relations were in prospect.

55

THE PUTIN DOCTRINE

Mr. Putin, senior Russian officials, and commentators have made their views of the post-cold-war order clear. In numerous statements Mr. Putin and other senior Russia officials have:

- Called for a Russian sphere of influence in the former Soviet space;
- Described Georgia, Ukraine, and now Kazakhstan as failed or artificial states;
- Asserted Moscow's right and even duty to protect not just ethnic Russians, but Russian speakers wherever they happen to reside. (Russian speakers make up 25 percent of the population of Kazakhstan; as well as our NATO allies Estonia and Latvia. There are also significant Russian populations in countries that used to be part of the Soviet Union.); and
- Called for new rules for the post-cold-war order, or "there will be no rules."

THE KREMLIN TOOL BOX FOR UNDERMINING THE PEACE OF EUROPE AND EURASIA

To understand the challenges posed by a country, it is necessary to understand not only its intention, but also its potential. To his credit, Mr. Putin has overseen the rebirth of a strong Russia. He has accomplished this by establishing some stability in the political system; instituting sound fiscal policies; permitting, within certain limits, entrepreneurs to make business decisions; and inviting Western investors. He was also a major beneficiary of the rise of gas and oil prices.

Mr. Putin presides over the world's sixth-largest economy. He controls one of the world's two-largest nuclear arsenals, the strongest conventional military in Europe, and the worlds' second-largest arms industry. In short, Mr. Putin's revisionist intentions are supported by a substantial economy—albeit one under pressure due to falling hydrocarbon prices—and one of the world's three most powerful militaries.

Were Moscow's attack on the post-cold-war order purely rhetorical, it would be problematic, but manageable. Unfortunately, this assault has been comprehensive. It involves Russia's information apparatus, intelligence services, criminal networks, business community, and military.

The heavily subsidized Russian media has been conducting a virulent anti-Western and particularly anti-American campaign for years. Mr. Putin's media have fanned xenophobia and intolerance throughout Russia. This campaign has been part of Mr. Putin's effort to (1) reduce the chance that the Russian people are attracted to democratic ideas, and (2) mobilize the Russian people to support his aggression in neighboring countries.

Russian intelligence services and connected criminal networks play an important part in Mr. Putin's efforts to undermine the post-cold-war order. First, we should note that the very organization of Moscow's intelligence agencies provides a clue to its intentions. The Soviet Union's intelligence service (the KGB) was split in half. The FSB was given responsibility for domestic security. The SVR was given responsibility for foreign intelligence. The fact that the independent states of the former Soviet Union were the responsibility of the FSB tells us what Moscow thinks of their independence.

A main purpose of the FSB—and the GRU, Russian military intelligence—is to penetrate the security organs of the neighboring states to ensure that they will promote Russian interests as defined by the Kremlin. That includes, as we have seen in Ukraine, making sure that the military, police, and intelligence will not mobilize against Russian-led insurrection or invasion.

Corruption, a major feature of Mr. Putin's Russia, is an important tool for the Kremlin in promoting its influence in the Near Abroad. The Kremlin understands that corrupt foreign officials are more pliant. Cooperation between Russian intelligence services and criminal organizations figures here. For instance, the siphoning off of vast resources from the gas sector into private hands has created a huge scandal in Russia and Ukraine. Shadowy companies—Eural Trans Gas, RosUkrEnergo—were set up as operators in a scheme put together by Semion Mogilevich, a major Russian crime boss.

As he consolidated power in Moscow, Mr. Putin established that Russian companies were subject to Kremlin control to promote objectives abroad. Gas and oil production is the heart of Russia's economy. Mr. Putin has used these assets to promote his foreign policy in a number of ways. He has built gas pipelines to Western Europe around Ukraine and even ally Belarus so that he can use gas as a weapon against these countries, while maintaining access to his wealthy customers in the West. He has hired shameless senior European officials to work as front men in his companies.

Gazprom has established business practices regarding the carrying of Central Asian gas in its pipelines and the delivery of gas to European customers that violate EU energy policy and maximizes Russian leverage in dealing with individual countries. For instance, Gazprom practices have made it harder for European countries to supply gas to Ukraine. This is done so that the Kremlin can punish Kyiv by cutting off the supply of gas. Lucrative arrangements with specific companies in select EU countries also build constituencies that will support Kremlin foreign policies.

As a last resort, of course, Mr. Putin has modernized and rebuilt the Russian military; and he has not hesitated to use it in pursuit of his revisionist objectives in Georgia and Ukraine.

THE KREMLIN RECORD BEFORE THE UKRAINE CRISIS

The crisis in Ukraine originated not in Ukraine, but in the minds of Mr. Putin and the Russian security elite that find the post-cold-war order unacceptable. While the broad extent of today's crisis is Mr. Putin's responsibility, its roots go back to imperialist thinking in Russian security circles since the dissolution of the Soviet Union.

In this respect, I commend to the committee Serhii Plokhy's excellent work, "The Last Empire: The Final Days of the Soviet Union." Dr. Plokhy describes how even Mikhail Gorbachev and Boris Yeltsin objected to Ukraine's 1991 referendum, in which 91 percent of the Ukrainians , including 54 percent in Crimea, voted for independence from the Soviet Union (and Russia). It is worth noting, too, that when the results of the Ukrainian referendum became clear, these two relatively liberal Russian politicians began to assert Moscow's right to protect Russians in Ukraine—the same "principle" that Mr. Putin has been using to justify his aggression.

From the very first days of the post-Soviet world, Moscow's security services developed the "frozen conflict" tactic to limit the sovereignty of its neighbors. It supported Armenian separatists in the Azerbaijan region of Nagorno-Karabakh in order to exert pressure on Azeris, South Ossetians, Ajarians, and the Abkhaz in Georgia to pressure Tbilisi, and the Slavs in Transnistria to keep Chisinau in check. For those who mistakenly blame current tensions with Moscow on the West, it is worth noting that Moscow had its frozen conflicts policy in place before discussions of NATO enlargement.

Russian activity in the Near Abroad in the 1990s was just a prelude to Mr. Putin's policies. He unleashed a massive cyber attack on Estonia in 2007 to express his unhappiness with a decision to take down a memorial to the Red Army in Tallinn. This attack took full advantage of the security service-criminal nexus in Russia described above. (Due to corruption, Russia, a nation rich in mathematicians, has not produced a world-class cyber company, but it does have the world's best hackers.). While it was clear that the attack in Estonia originated in Moscow, the West chose not to state this clearly or to make it an issue in its relationship with Mr. Putin.

In 2008, Moscow provoked a conflict with Georgian President Mikheil Saakashvili and used its army to defeat the Georgian military. In that same year, Moscow recognized Georgia's breakaway regions as independent. Moscow's aggression was condemned in the West, albeit to varying degrees. It is both amusing and sad to note in retrospect that then-French President Nicolas Sarkozy agreed to sell Moscow the Mistral aircraft carrier as a reward for observing the cease-fire that he had negotiated.

This episode revealed a weakness of Western diplomacy toward Russia that Mr. Putin has been exploiting regularly in the current Ukrainian crisis. Mr. Putin commits an act of aggression, threatens further aggression, and then graciously accepts Western gifts in exchange for not escalating the violence. While the American response to Mr. Putin's aggression was not craven, President Obama launched his naive reset with Mr. Putin only a year after the Georgian war.

MR. PUTIN'S UKRAINE ADVENTURE AND THE WEST'S REACTION

Mr. Putin's adventure in Ukraine began when he decided at some point in 2013 that it would be unacceptable for Ukraine to sign a trade agreement with the EU. This prospect had not disturbed him in the past. When I served as Ambassador in Ukraine, it was clear that Moscow strongly opposed NATO membership for Ukraine, but it had not taken a position against EU membership for the country. And of course, the prospective trade agreement was a good deal short of membership. It is important to remember this when reading the arguments of those who claim that this crisis is actually due to NATO enlargement.

Most Ukrainians, including then President Yanukovych, who was often described as pro-Kremlin (a simplification), wanted the EU deal. Partly due to Kremlin pressure—Moscow had been banning Ukrainian exports—Mr. Yanukovych backed away from the trade deal in late November 2013. The next day, there were tens of thousands of demonstrators on the streets of Kyiv protesting this decision. When Mr.

Yanukovych tried to clear the streets with strong-arm policing, he roused hundreds of thousands of demonstrators, tired of his corrupt and increasingly authoritarian rule. Mr. Putin's offers of lower gas prices and a loan of $15 billion did not satisfy the demonstrators. For 2 months Mr. Yanukovych alternated between police methods and inadequate concessions to persuade the protestors to go home. He failed. Sergei Glaziyev, Mr. Putin's principal adviser on Ukraine, was publicly urging Mr. Yanukovych to use force to deal with the protesters.

Finally in late February 2014, Mr. Yanukovych either permitted or ordered the use of sniper fire to terrorize the protesters into leaving the streets. A hundred people died as a result. But the demonstrators did not leave the streets; they were enraged and Mr. Yanukovych's political support collapsed. He fled the country a few days later for Russia.

In response, the Kremlin launched its invasion of Crimea with ''little green men,'' who looked like and were equipped like Russian soldiers, but without the insignias and flags of the Russian military. The United States and Europe placed some mild economic sanctions on Russia in response. They were also making every effort in private diplomacy and public statements to offer Mr. Putin an ''off ramp'' for the crisis. That the West had such a tender regard for Mr. Putin's dignity was not unnoticed in the Kremlin and certainly made Mr. Putin's decision to launch his hybrid war in the Donbass easier. The Sarkozy model was holding and has yet to be broken.

Since Mr. Putin launched his decreasingly covert war in Ukraine's East, he has escalated his intervention several times. It began last April with Russian leadership, arms, and money. When Ukraine launched its counteroffensive under newly elected President Poroshenko last June, the Kremlin sent in increasingly sophisticated weapons (including the missile system that shot down the Malaysian airliner in July), more mercenaries (including the Vostok Battalion of Chechens), and finally the Russian Army itself in August. Only the use of regular Russian forces stopped the Ukrainian counteroffensive. Throughout this period, the West was slow and weak in confronting the Kremlin. For instance, the G–7 leaders had warned Mr. Putin in early June that if he did not cease his intervention in Ukraine by the end of the month, Russia would face sectoral sanctions. Yet by the end of June, despite the introduction of major Russian weapons systems into Ukraine, there was no more talk of sectoral sanctions. Only the downing of the Malaysian passenger jet in July and the invasion by Russian troops persuaded the Europeans to put those sanctions in place.

After the regular Russian forces defeated the Ukrainian Army in early September, Germany and France helped negotiate the Minsk I cease-fire. However, Russia repeatedly violated its agreement by introducing more military equipment and supplies into Ukraine and taking an additional 500 square kilometers of Ukrainian territory. This escalated aggression did not lead to any additional sanctions last year.

Despite the Russian offensive that greeted the New Year, EU foreign policy chief Mogherini was floating the idea of easing sanctions. As the violence increased, Ms. Mogherini dropped the subject. But in February, Germany and France helped negotiate a new cease-fire, Minsk II, with terms far worse for Ukraine. Mr. Putin certainly enjoyed this process. The Sarkozy pattern was unbroken. For violating Minsk I, Mr. Putin received a much more favorable cease-fire, which he promptly violated by seizing the strategic town of Debaltseve. And why not? While Western leaders huff and puff at each new Kremlin aggression, they hope out loud that this is the last one. And then, occasionally they levy additional sanctions on Russia.

### WHAT THE WEST SHOULD EXPECT NEXT FROM THE KREMLIN

Nowhere has Mr. Putin stated clearly what he needs to stop his war against Ukraine. Western leaders have fallen all over themselves offering solutions publicly and privately to assuage the Russian strongman, but to no avail. There is a simple reason for this. Mr. Putin's objective in Ukraine is, at a maximum, to establish a compliant regime in Kyiv. This is something that he cannot achieve, because a large majority of Ukrainian citizens despise him for the bloody war that he unleashed. His minimum objective is to destabilize the country, so that it cannot effectively reform itself and orient its policy toward Europe.

Mr. Putin has not stated these objectives formally, because they are things he cannot admit in polite society. But destabilizing Ukraine means that he cannot sit still in the territories that have already been conquered by his proxies. He has to continually stir the pot by military action and/or terrorism/subversion. A good example of terror was the bombs set off in Kharkiv that killed demonstrators at last month's rally honoring those killed by snipers on Kyiv's Maidan Square.

Leaders in Washington, London, Berlin, and Paris need to understand what their counterparts in Warsaw, Riga, Tallinn, and Vilnius understand: that Kremlin ambitions go beyond Ukraine. If the West does not stop Mr. Putin now, they will find him revising the post-cold-war order elsewhere. It is time to break the Sarkozy pattern.

Mr. Putin is not hiding his ambitions. While we do not know precisely where he may move next, we know the candidates. The Kremlin has proclaimed its right to a sphere of influence throughout the post-Soviet space, as well as its right to protect ethnic Russians and Russian-speakers wherever they reside. This just happens to include the entire post-Soviet space, including some countries that were never part of the Soviet Union, but were members of the Warsaw Pact. Kazakhstan's Russian-speaking Slavic community is 25 percent of its population. The same is true in Estonia and Latvia.

Last August, Mr. Putin called Kazakhstan an artificial country created by the genius of President Nazarbayev. Mr. Putin noted that Russians in Kazakhstan faced no ill treatment under President Nazarbayev, but speculated that problems could arise once he passes the scene. Kazakhstan's Slavs are located along the border with Russia, in areas that contain a good percentage of the country's oil resources. Just as the West's weak reaction to Moscow's Georgian invasion emboldened Mr. Putin to strike in Ukraine, so too will a Western-tolerated Kremlin victory in Ukraine endanger the former states of the Soviet Union. Is that an acceptable outcome for Western statesmen?

The danger goes beyond the grey zone, to states that enjoy membership in the EU and NATO. While never recognized by the United States, Estonia, Latvia, and Lithuania were incorporated into the Soviet Union; and two of those states have large Slavic communities. A good number of serious thinkers and statesmen say that Mr. Putin's reach will not extend to the Baltic States, because they are members of NATO and have Article 5 protection under the NATO Charter. That is, of course, a critical deterrent, but does Mr. Putin understand this?

Mr. Putin has wondered publicly, as have other senior Russian officials, why NATO is still in existence. After all, they opine, it was created to stop the Soviet Union, which dissolved 25 years ago. It is no secret that the Kremlin would like to weaken the alliance. Mr. Putin has been playing games in the Baltics to probe for weaknesses and to challenge the applicability of Article 5. The list is not small. In 2007, he unleashed the devastating cyber attack on Estonia. Last September, on the day that the NATO summit ended (2 days after the visit of President Obama to Tallinn), the Kremlin seized an Estonian counterintelligence officer from Estonia. A few weeks later, Russia seized a Lithuanian ship from international waters in the Baltic Sea.

## WHAT THE UNITED STATES AND THE WEST MUST DO

First, Western leaders need to understand the nature of Mr. Putin's threat. In charge of one of the world's most formidable militaries and a large economy, he is intent on upsetting the post-cold-war order. He represents a threat to global order far larger than ISIL, and notably larger than a radical-Mullah-run Iran seeking nuclear weapons. NATO statesmen who labeled ISIL and not Russia an existential threat to the alliance will be figures of fun for future historians.

Recognizing this means that we will cease to take seriously the argument that we must let Mr. Putin violate the sovereignty of multiple neighbors in order to get his help with Iran and ISIL. It would also mean that we would spend more resources dealing with the Kremlin menace than we devote to ISIL.

This last point is especially important in the intelligence area. The intelligence resources that we devote to an aggressive nuclear superpower is significantly less than what we use to monitor a rag tag bunch of terrorists numbering no more than 20,000. It also matters when looking at financial and military support for Ukraine, as we will discuss below.

If we understand that Mr. Putin's ambitions extend to the entire post-Soviet space, including perhaps our Baltic NATO allies, we recognize that we have significant interest in stopping Mr. Putin's aggression in Ukraine. We do not want Mr. Putin's grasping hand extending to additional countries, and we have a vital interest in stopping him if he moves against Estonia, Latvia, or Lithuania. It is very much in our interest to make his life so uncomfortable in Ukraine that the Kremlin thinks twice about additional aggression.

First, on Ukraine.

## SANCTIONS

In Ukraine, our short- and middle-term objectives should be to prevent further Russian aggression, which will allow President Poroshenko to reform and develop Ukraine in peace. That is not easy to do, since Mr. Putin's plan is precisely the opposite, to keep the pot boiling. Our policy should not be to refrain from taking any ''provocative'' action, in the hopes that this time the Kremlin will actually observe the Minsk II cease-fire. This approach has failed multiple times for over a year. It guarantees that the crisis will escalate, because the only world leader who believes that there is a military solution to the Ukraine crisis has an office in Red Square.

To increase the odds that Mr. Putin does not move beyond the current cease-fire line, we must address his vulnerabilities. He has at least two. First of all, his implicit deal with the Russian people is that he delivers prosperity and they let him rule the country. The Russian economy is under serious pressure today because of the sectoral sanctions levied last summer by the United States and EU, in addition to the sharp fall of hydrocarbon prices. The sanctions will bite harder with time, especially if oil prices remain low.

The last serious sanctions were put in place lasts September. Since then, Moscow has taken over 500 square kilometers of additional Ukrainian territory and violated both the Minsk I and II cease-fires. For that, both the United States and the EU should either level additional sectoral sanctions or extend last year's sectoral sanctions. In response to the latest Kremlin aggression, the EU renewed some sanctions imposed last spring early. That was not enough. Besides additional major sanctions for the substantial aggression over the past 6 months, it is time for the United States and Europe to take the initiative. Specifically, they should reach agreement on new sanctions that will be imposed if the Kremlin's proxies seize Mariupol or any additional territory in Ukraine. This might serve as a deterrent for the Kremlin.

Part of this deterrent could include a public discussion of removing Russia from the SWIFT system of financial payments. Actually barring Russia from SWIFT would have a devastating impact on Moscow's economy; it would also be controversial globally. But an effort by the United States to put it on the agenda would create substantial pressure on Moscow and encourage the Europeans to be less cautious in applying additional sectoral sanctions.

It is important to note here that the Obama administration has done a good job in regards to sanctions. It understands that the key to success is to make sure that both the United States and the EU sanction Russia. I fully understand that there is reluctance in corners of the EU to do so. The administration has worked hard, and largely with success, to impose sanctions in tandem with Europe. But as described above, the process has been too slow.

## MILITARY ASSISTANCE

Mr. Putin's second vulnerability concerns the use of his army in Ukraine. While his media have spread a sea of vitriol among the people of Russia, it has not been able to persuade them that Russian troops should be used in Ukraine. Since last summer, numerous polls by Moscow's Levada Center have shown that a large majority of the Russian people oppose using troops in Ukraine. Since his people do not want Russian troops in Ukraine, he is telling them that no troops are there. He is lying to his people. Thousands of regular Russian troops were used in August and September to stop Ukraine's counteroffensive. Our intelligence now estimates that there are anywhere from 250 to 1,000 Russian officers in Ukraine. Ukrainian intelligence claims that there are as many as 9,000 or 10,000 Russian troops in Ukraine. I am not endorsing the higher figures. I do believe, however, that since we are not devoting enough intelligence assets to the Russia menace, our numbers are far from certain; and if they err, it is likely on the low side.

In any case, Russian casualties are a vulnerability for Mr. Putin. He is burying his dead in secret. More casualties make this harder to do. What this amounts to, is that we should give Ukraine defensive, lethal aid, so that is may defend itself.

I was one of a group of eight former U.S. officials who issued a report urging the Obama administration to provide $1 billion in defensive arms, including lethal equipment, to Ukraine for the next 3 years. For a major national security priority, $1 billion a year is not a great deal of money. In the first 6 months of Operation Inherent Resolve against ISIL, the United States spent $1.5 billion.

The purpose is to deter further aggression—and to stabilize the situation in the rest of Ukraine. Opponents of this idea argue that this would not deter the Mr. Putin, because the Kremlin has escalation advantage, and Ukraine is more important to Russia than the United States. It may be true that Ukraine is more important to Moscow than Washington, but it is not more important to Moscow than to

Kyiv. Kyiv and the Ukrainian people will continue to fight the aggressors. Why do we want to disadvantage the victim of aggression by denying them arms?

Some opponents of providing weapons argue that Kremlin military strength means that it can defeat any weapons system we provide. And if that happens, it would be geopolitical defeat for the United States. This is simply false. We can pursue a policy of weapons supply without taking responsibility for securing Moscow's defeat. We can provide weapons while making clear that we have no intention of using American troops. This was the successful rationale behind the Reagan Doctrine, which challenged Soviet overreach in Third World conflicts around the globe by providing weapons.

The last point is this. If we understand that Mr. Putin's aim of revising the post-cold-war order may mean aggression in countries beyond Ukraine, it is very much in our interest to make his experience in Ukraine as painful as possible. That will make him more vulnerable at home and will leave him with fewer resources for mischief elsewhere.

The Obama administration is reviewing its position on weapons for Ukraine. Many senior figures in the administration support this. It is time for the White House to make the decision to send weapons to Ukraine. Chancellor Merkel made clear during her visit to Washington last month, that while she opposes the supply of weapons to Ukraine, she would work to ensure that such a decision by the United States did not undermine transatlantic unity.

Such military equipment must include light antiarmor weapons—the massing of Russian tanks was critical as Moscow's proxies seized Debaltseve in violation of Minsk II—and counterbattery radar for long range missiles. Seventy percent of Ukrainian casualties come from missile and artillery fire. The report also recommends sending armored Humvees, secure communications equipment, equipment to jam Russian unmanned aerial vehicles, and medical supplies.

Within the U.S. Government, Congress has taken the lead on the supply of weapons for Ukraine, when it passed the Ukraine Freedom Support Act. That bill authorized the expenditure of USD 340M for weapons. Congress may need to act once again. But this time it is essential to pass legislation that both authorizes and appropriates USD 3B over 3 years. This is the most pressing national security danger at the moment. Congress needs to appropriate resources.

There is also a critical economic element in the Ukraine crisis. This involves both comprehensive reform in Ukraine and Western assistance to help Ukraine pay its short-term international debt. I have not dwelt on this here because this testimony focusses on the broader Kremlin danger. But it is important to note that the West needs strongly encourage the Poroshenko/Yatsenyuk team to implement reform and provide the necessary financing on the debt problem.

In addition, while focusing on stabilizing the security situation in Ukraine's East, the West must not recognize in any way Moscow's annexation of Crimea. The United States and Europe can support the people of Crimea by:

- Maintaining the sanctions already passed in response to the Kremlin's taking of Crimea;
- Refusing to confer legitimacy on Moscow's control of Crimea, just as the United States refused accept the to recognize the Soviet Union's ''incorporation'' of the Baltic States after the signing of the Molotov-Ribbentrop Pact;
- Passing legislation forbidding its citizens and companies from conducting business with Russian authorities and companies in Crimea, except when the Government of Ukraine agrees;
- Making sure that their courts are open to suits by the government, companies, and citizens of Ukraine for the use of Crimean assets and resources by the Russian Government and others not authorized by the government of Ukraine.

COUNTERING REVISIONISM BEYOND UKRAINE

The United States must act in two different geopolitical areas beyond Ukraine to deal with Moscow's revanchist tendencies. Most importantly, we must act decisively to strengthen NATO and deterrence in the new members of the alliance, especially the Baltic States. Since the Kremlin offensive in Ukraine's East began last spring, NATO has taken a number of positive steps in this direction. Last April, the Pentagon deployed infantry units of 150 troops to Poland, Estonia, Latvia, and Lithuania. This is a ''persistent,'' but rotating deployment. Washington is also planning on deploying 150 Abrams tanks and Bradley fighting vehicles to Poland. Air patrols in the Baltic States have tripled in the past year. And more NATO ships are entering the Black Sea than in the past.

These are all good measures. So too was the decision at the Wales summit to create a rapid response force that could deploy 5,000 soldiers within 48 hours; and the decision by NATO Defense Ministers last month to place some headquarters' functions in Bulgaria, Romania, Poland, and the Baltic States.

Still, two more steps are needed in the short term. First the deployment thus far is too small. During the cold war, our "trip wire" force in Germany was 200,000 troops. We should put forward in the Baltics at least a fully equipped battalion. Of even more importance, we need a quickly but carefully worked contingency plan for the appearance of Kremlin provocateurs among the Slavic population of Estonia or Latvia. This plan should include elements for small provocations, such as the kidnapping of the Estonian intelligence official. We should also work within the alliance to achieve agreement to formally review the NATO–Russia Founding Act if Moscow's proxies seize significant territory in Ukraine.

The second area that requires a new policy is that grey zone in Eastern Europe, the Caucasus, and Central Asia where Moscow claims a sphere of influence. Do Western policymakers believe that Moscow has a right to order things in this area as it chooses—never mind the preferences of the other states? If not, the United States, NATO, and the EU need to consider measures that will strengthen these countries. Some are relatively simple. Countries interested in a stronger United States and/or NATO security connection would certainly welcome more American or NATO military visits. For Georgia that might mean more port visits by a more proactive NATO presence in the Black Sea. In Central Asia, that might mean more CENTCOM visits for Uzbekistan. We might enhance cooperation with all interested Central Asian states in offsetting the potential destabilizing impact of our withdrawal from Afghanistan. While this may seem counterintuitive, this last initiative need not exclude the Kremlin. Indeed we can also help strengthen some nations on Russia's periphery by projects that include the Kremlin. This would also demonstrate that our policies are designed not just to discourage Kremlin aggression, but also to seek cooperation on matters of mutual interest.

Policy in the grey zone should also focus on state weaknesses that Moscow exploits in order to exert its control. As discussed above, the Kremlin uses its intelligence services to recruit agents in the power ministries of the post-Soviet states; and its uses its firms to acquire key sectors' of these countries' economies and to buy political influence. With interested countries, the United States and NATO should offer programs to help vet the security services and military in order to establish that they are under the full control of the political leaders in these states. At the same time, the United States and the EU offer programs to uncover corruption in the financial and other sectors' of these countries' economies.

### A FINAL POLICY RECOMMENDATION

There is one more element of Mr. Putin's aggressive policy that needs to be addressed: the weaponization of information. An admitted admirer of Nazi propagandist Joseph Goebbels, Mr. Putin has gained nearly complete control over the Russian media and turned it into an instrument promoting extreme nationalism. Its disinformation has been successful especially at home, but also in neighboring countries. The budget for broadcasts by Radio Free Europe and Radio Liberty in Russian and other languages of the former Soviet Empire was sharply curtailed after the dissolution of the Soviet Union. At the time, that made sense. It no longer does.

In response to the crisis in Ukraine, the Broadcasting Board of Governors (BBG) in FY15 increased its budget for Russian-language programming by 49 percent to USD 23.2M. It will be asking for an additional USD 15.4M for FY 2016. I would certainly endorse this request for additional funds, but would also suggest that Congress reach out to the BBG to see if, in fact, more resources are not required.

### A KREMLIN PROBLEM, NOT A RUSSIA PROBLEM

The challenge that we face is rooted in Mr. Putin's style of leadership, a style which privileges the security services, with their neoimperial policy preferences, criminal connections, and disdain for civil society and democracy. None of the policies recommended in this paper are directed against the people of Russia. The assassination of Boris Nemtsov last month is a reminder of a truth uttered by the great Russian historian, Vasiliy Klyuchevskiy, in his lectures on Russian history. He observed that the expansion of the Russian state abroad is inversely proportional to the development of freedom for the Russian people. In other words, expansion abroad means repression at home. That is certainly the pattern that Mr. Putin has established. Opposing Mr. Putin's aggressive policies is not only vital to our national security, but a service for the Russian people as well.

The CHAIRMAN. Thank you both for outstanding testimony.

And I am going to defer questions at this moment to Senator Menendez.

Senator MENENDEZ. Well, thank you, Mr. Chairman. And thank you both for your service to our country at different times.

It is always a pleasure to welcome another Tennessean here to the hearing room. You have a great Tennessean here as the chairman, and you should all be very proud of him.

Ambassador Herbst, let me just ask you. I think you laid out a pretty compelling case and probably did it better than I have been successful in trying to do in terms of the importance of it. You spent time in Kyiv as our Ambassador. You had a lot of opportunities to observe President Putin's behavior toward its neighbors. If I were to ask you to—and you have largely, I think, already referred to his intentions, but would you expect, for example, if unchecked, Russian forces to move into Mariupol?

Ambassador HERBST. Mr. Putin cannot accept a frozen conflict. A frozen conflict is a bad outcome. But with a frozen conflict, Ukraine could develop as a democratic, prosperous state, and that is what Mr. Putin is against. So he has to move beyond the area he currently controls.

Mariupol is the most likely target but not the only one. He could move further into the northern parts of the Donbass. The Russians have been conducting a terror campaign in Kharkiv. Kharkiv is arguably the second largest city in the whole country, but the Russians have been unable to establish a clear presence there. But they will continue to probe there. They will move wherever they can with the least casualties to themselves and the least uproar in Europe. We need to provide Ukraine the means to stop that from happening. Otherwise, Mr. Putin will continue to go forward.

Senator MENENDEZ. Let me ask you to answer two questions that are also often poised in a contrary view to mine, that providing defensive lethal weapons to Ukraine would create serious problems with Europe or that providing such weapons would just lead Russia to further escalate. What would you say in response to those questions?

Ambassador HERBST. I will start with the second because the answer is quicker. Mr. Putin has escalated half a dozen times precisely because he has not had any pushback. If we push back, I am not going to say Mr. Putin will not escalate. We do not know what he will do. But the chances of him escalating go down. That is the second question.

As for the first question, I watched very carefully Chancellor Merkel's visit to Washington in February. She said ''that she opposes sending weapons to Ukraine.'' She also said that if the United States were to do that, she would work hard to make sure that there is no transatlantic disharmony. That is an amber light, a light which we can go through because she understands the United States may ultimately make the intelligent decision to provide Ukraine the weapons needed to defend itself. I do not have any doubt that we can manage the alliance on this issue. What you need is strong leadership, which unfortunately we have not seen, strong leadership from Washington in Europe, in NATO. With that, this is manageable.

Senator MENENDEZ. Thank you, Mr. Chairman.

The CHAIRMAN. Well, gentlemen, I apologize for not having questions at this moment. I have got to get to a meeting at 12:45. This has been a very long, but a very informative meeting. I want to thank you both for your testimony, and if you would, we will have some written questions we would like for you to respond to.

I do think the strategy that you have laid out, Ambassador, is very clear, very helpful. I think, Ambassador Kornblum, the insights into what is driving Russia were also very helpful. We appreciate both of you for your service to our country, for being here as an asset to us as we try to serve our country.

And with that, the record for this hearing will be open until March the 12th. So if people have questions, they can send those in and hopefully you will respond promptly to those.

We thank you again for being here.

The meeting is adjourned.

[Whereupon, at 12:38 p.m., the hearing was adjourned.]

---

### ADDITIONAL MATERIAL SUBMITTED FOR THE RECORD

#### PREPARED STATEMENT OF OLEXANDER MOTSYK, AMBASSADOR OF UKRAINE

Distinguished Senators, ladies and gentlemen, let me start with expression of gratitude for your continued support of Ukraine in this difficult time of its young history. Last year was a period of unprecedented challenges to global order and international law, which Russian aggression against my country brought about. But it was also a time of strong unity of the civilized world in the face of fundamental threat to democracy and peace.

This threat has emerged as a response to aspirations of the Ukrainian nation to return to its European roots. The Revolution of Dignity on Kyiv's Maidan has evoked admiration around the globe as an unbreakable ambition to break with the past and strive for prosperous future. At the same time, it was perceived as an existential threat by the Russian leadership which deems liberty and democracy as obstacles on a path to realization of its goals.

A year of Russian aggression has undeniably revealed the true intentions of Moscow's actions. Its persistence in spite of Western sanctions and international isolation shows that Russia will use any means necessary to forestall democratic development of Ukraine. The primary goal is to prevent Ukraine's European integration, keep it in Russia's orbit, or dismember it altogether.

The Kremlin uses any means to fulfill this task, including the attempted illegal annexation of our sovereign territory of Crimea, manufacturing conflict, based on false pretext, in eastern Ukraine and directly participating in it by flooding the region with weapons, military equipment, mercenaries, Russian armed forces and resorting to vicious propaganda campaign.

The character of Russia's geopolitical calculation show that despite the central role of Ukraine, it is only one of the key elements in the implementation of its strategic objective—restoration of new form of the Soviet Union by creating a circle of instability in the region. In the 21st century, when progress is achieved through cooperation and measured by well-being, Russia resorts to force, coercion, intimidation, and violation of international law as the means of imposing its will on the global arena. Chances are high that this line of action will not be limited to Ukraine and will reach other countries such as Moldova, Georgia, and Kazakhstan, and even NATO allies, primarily the Baltic States.

In defense of their land, Ukrainians demonstrated an unswerving will to protect their country. This fight, however, is not only about us. By countering the forces of oppression and authoritarianism, Ukraine serves as a powerful line of defense of freedom and democracy. Our success in this struggle today is the guarantee that the full-scale war will not come knocking on the doors of the West tomorrow.

We highly appreciate great support of the United States, both the administration and U.S. Congress, provided so far. Without it, the situation for our independence would be much more difficult. A number of declarative and legislative actions by Congress have created a formidable framework of cooperation between our countries in general, and in countering the Russian aggression in particular. Combined with strong stand and decisive action by the administration, they established the leading role of the United States in this process and reinforced the unity with Europe as a major factor in its success.

Despite the strong counteraction, Russia's calculus remains unchanged and the efforts to restore the vision of Europe whole, free, and at peace must be enhanced. In this context, we want to hope for full implementation of Freedom Support Act, passed by the U.S. Congress last year, which envisages a number of provisions, fulfillment of which would significantly impact the situation.

Ukraine shares the view of its Western partners that the diplomatic settlement is the only way forward in terms of resolving the conflict. But we also believe that a decision in favor of providing Ukraine with means to defend itself would considerably contribute to this process. The concerns associated with such a step are legitimate, but there can be no doubt that defensive weapons in possession of Ukraine would substantially raise the cost of Russian aggression. They would incline Moscow to negotiate or at least waive any remaining doubts about its strategic intentions.

Ukraine will not use arms to escalate the conflict. Our goal is to bring peace to our people. That is why last month at the Minsk summit, Ukraine negotiated an agreement with Russia, with the participation of Germany and France. Although extremely fragile, the deal can lay a reliable foundation for a peaceful settlement of the conflict. Our major concern in this regard is the inclination of the Russian side and the separatists it supports to comply with their obligations.

The seizure of Debaltsevo, the increasing threat of attack on Mariupol and the continued flooding of Ukraine's territory with Russian weapons and military personnel raise doubts about Moscow's inclination to implement the Minsk Agreement. If these activities continue, the response of the West has to be robust with all options on the table. These can include traditional means of raising the cost for aggression, such as new round of economic sanction, but also new measures—exclusion of Russia from international organizations and SWIFT banking system, and deprivation of the right to host the 2018 FIFA World Cup.

Moscow has to be put before a simple choice: either it will comply with international law or suffer difficult consequences. In order for good relations to be restored, Russian forces, mercenraries, and arms must leave Ukraine's territory and the Kremlin must stop its interference in our internal affairs. Restoration of territorial integrity of Ukraine must be seen as a logical step in the context of Budapest Memorandum, of which Russia is the side.

This also concerns the Ukrainian region of Crimea, which has become the victim of the initial stage of Russian aggression. Since the unlawful annexation of peninsula it has turned into a territory of brutal violations of human rights and abuses of individual freedoms. The indegeneous population of Crimean Tatars is constantly harassed by the puppet authorities, while the mere of expression of support for Ukraine is treated as a crime. We believe that this situation can be resolved only through return of Crimea to Ukraine and we will not rest until this goal is achieved.

Although preservation of territorial integrity dominates on Ukraine's agenda, other challenges are of critical implication as well. We are determined to use the chance of truce presented by the Minsk Agreement to make progress with much-needed reforms in our country. As of today, Ukrainian Government and Verkhovna Rada took significant steps directed at comprehensive overhaul of the state budget, judicial system, prosecutor's office, pension system, anticorruption legislation, energy-efficiency, governmental transparency. This incomplete list will be expanded as the Ukrainians are committed to transforming their country into a modern European state.

Progress in this area would not have been possible without strong financial support of our Western partners led by the United States. We hope that this support will be expanded into a comprehensive program similar to the Marshall Plan, which once helped Europe to recover from the consequences of a devastating war.

For all the tragedy of recent developments in Ukraine, they have demonstrated that in face of enormous challenges, the Ukrainians have chosen not to give in but to stand up for their rights and freedoms, and to unite to preserve their country's sovereignty. What can be observed today is the reemergence of a new civilized European nation, determined to build its future on the everlasting principles of accountable government, respect for human rights, dynamic civil society, free media and protected national security. It is my strong conviction that sooner rather than later this development will lead us to become an equal and effective member of the European family of nations.

Such an outcome would be in the interests of not only the Ukrainian people, but also of Europe as a whole, including Russia. This task can be fulfilled through strong and decisive actions of the democratic world aimed at assisting Ukraine, restoring the stability of international system and negating the prospects of another global conflict. We are looking forward to the continued U.S. leadership in this process.

---

RESPONSES OF VICTORIA NULAND TO QUESTIONS
SUBMITTED BY SENATOR BOB CORKER

*Question.* Although the terms of Minsk II cease-fire agreement indicate that Debaltseve should remain part of Ukrainian-held territory, the Russian-backed rebels launched an offensive to acquire the town after they signed the cease-fire agreement and now control Debaltseve.

♦ What does this indicate about the commitment of the rebels to the Minsk agreement and its implementation? Is it the position of the administration that the rebels will have to withdraw from Debaltseve? What is the deadline for this withdrawal?

Answer. Combined Russian-separatist forces launched the offensive on Debaltseve before the negotiations in Minsk on the February 12, 2015, Minsk implementation plan—also called ''Minsk II'' by some—and extended the offensive through the negotiations, leading to the Ukrainians' withdrawal of their forces from Debaltseve on February 18. The September 2014 Minsk agreements have the line of contact running clearly east of Debaltseve, leaving that city firmly in the Ukrainian Government's hands. The February 12 Minsk implementation plan links back to those agreements. We support Ukraine's claim that Debaltseve lies outside the Special Status Area, and that the separatists must vacate it as part of the fulfillment of the Minsk agreements.

The commitments contained within the Minsk agreements are supposed to be fulfilled by the end of 2015, but this will require political will on the part of Ukraine, Russia, and the Russia-backed separatists, all of whom signed the agreements. We stand ready to assist in their fulfillment, as we believe the Minsk agreements are the best chance for a durable, diplomatic resolution of the crisis. We will judge the separatists and their Russian backers by their actions.

*Question.* What distinguishes the second Minsk cease-fire agreement from the first? Why would this cease-fire agreement hold when the first cease-fire agreement collapsed?

Answer. The main distinguishing feature to date has been the overall reduction of violence along the cease-fire line since the February 15 cease-fire went into effect.

That said, attacks across the cease-fire line persist, and their numbers have recently increased. The OSCE's Special Monitoring Mission (SMM) has been inhibited by access restrictions placed on it mainly by the Russia-backed separatists, making it difficult for the SMM to report on cease-fire violations and the status of heavy weapons withdrawal. We have seen frequent attacks usually initiated by the separatists against Ukrainian positions to the west and north of the cease-fire line.

A true cease-fire would require full and unfettered access by the OSCE SMM to the entire length of the cease-fire line and separatist-held territory, and constant vigilance by the U.S., our European allies and partners, and like-minded countries.

We must be prepared to increase the costs on Russia and the separatists if we see continued stalling on fulfillment of the Minsk commitments, or renewed land grabs by combined Russian-separatist forces.

*Question.* The Minsk II agreement states that Ukraine will not be able to assume control of its internationally recognized border with Russia until Kyiv changes its constitution to include decentralization. Is decentralization clearly defined in the agreement?

Answer. Decentralization is defined sufficiently in the Minsk agreements—including the February 12 Minsk implementation plan, or ''Minsk II''—that it should be achievable to a standard that is agreeable to all concerned. It will be complicated, however, as the process of decentralization applies to the entire country of Ukraine, and therefore will require the agreement of the Ukrainian Parliament (Rada) on its features, not only for the area currently held by the separatists, but for all of Ukraine. We are confident the Ukrainian Government and Rada can find a solution that will work and have the desired effect.

RESPONSES OF BRIAN P. MCKEON TO QUESTIONS
SUBMITTED BY SENATOR BOB CORKER

### TRAINING THE UKRAINIAN NATIONAL GUARD

*Question.* Why have plans to train Ukrainian National Guard troops not been implemented?

Answer. DOD and the Department of State notified Congress last summer of the administration's intent to transfer a total of $19 million of available fiscal year (FY) 2014 funds to the Global Security Contingency Fund for the purpose of providing training and additional nonlethal equipment to units of the Ukrainian National Guard as early as the second quarter of FY 2015. The equipment will begin arriving in early April and the training is scheduled to begin the week of 20 April.

### DELAYS IN NONLETHAL MILITARY ASSISTANCE

*Question.* Approximately $120 million in nonlethal military assistance has been committed to Ukraine by the United States but equipment worth only half of this amount has been delivered this Ukraine. What explain this delay?

Answer. Ukraine is a top priority and we are working to further expedite the provision of assistance. When implementing government-to-government security assistance programs, however, we must operate through technology, security, and foreign disclosure reviews; contracting processes; and then arrange for transportation and delivery. We are constantly working to speed up these timelines and have been successful in some instances, such as countermortar radars, which we were able to deliver these in less than 2 months after the decision was made to provide them. We will continue to expedite the provision of assistance whenever possible. Once the GSCF training program starts in late April for the Ukrainian National Guard, we will have delivered well over half of the $120 million in assistance.

### ASSESSMENT OF UKRAINIAN CAPACITY, CAPABILITIES AND GAPS

*Question.* Has the U.S. military conducted an assessment of the Ukrainian Armed Forces to gain an understanding of their current capacity, capabilities, and gaps? What were the findings and how is the United States prepared to assist in filling the training and arming gaps?

Answer. Yes, through the U.S.-Ukraine Joint Commission, led by the U.S. European Command and senior Ukrainian Ministry of Defense officials, the United States engages in regular, senior-level discussions with Ukraine to identify gaps in Ukraine's military capacity and capability. Over the past year, the Joint Commission conducted comprehensive assessments of Ukrainian military functional areas. These assessments resulted in prioritized lists of requirements that have informed current security assistance, mid- and long-term cooperative and institutional reform efforts, and training and professionalization of the Ukrainian Armed Forces. The assessment teams have made recommendations for improvements and growth in the following areas: medical, logistics, institution building, special operations, communications, information, and border security. The assessment and review process, through the commission, is an ongoing process

### NECESSARY EQUIPMENT FOR THE UKRAINIAN MILITARY

*Question.* Does the Ukrainian military possess the necessary equipment, including lethal weapons systems, to effectively respond to attacks from the Russian-backed rebels and Russian forces operating in eastern Ukraine or neighboring Russian regions? What U.S. weapons systems and equipment, if provided, would pay the biggest return on investment—lethal and nonlethal? What is the status of providing such equipment?

Answer. We do not believe a military resolution of this conflict is possible. The President is regularly reviewing options to support Ukraine, including whether the United States should provide defensive lethal assistance. We have thus far provided assistance that helps to address key Ukrainian capability gaps, such as in communications, mobility, and countermortar radars. We continue to provide assistance to Ukraine and expect deliveries to continue for at least the next 18 months as funds are allocated, contracts signed, and equipment delivered. We are also processing $75 million in additional assistance authorized as part of the European Reassurance Initiative (ERI).

RESPONSES OF JOHN C. KORNBLUM TO QUESTIONS
SUBMITTED BY SENATOR BOB CORKER

*Question.* What exactly is at stake for the United States in Ukraine? What are the consequences of our failure and Putin's success?

Answer. Russian action against Ukraine came almost exactly 20 years after Russia, together with the U.S., U.K. and France had guaranteed the sovereignty and territorial integrity of Ukraine as part of Ukraine's relinquishment of nuclear weapons it had inherited from the Soviet Union. Ukraine's independence and security were thus tied to the overall "settlement" of issues resulting from the collapse of the USSR. For the United States to acquiesce in Russia's unilateral moves against Ukraine, would mean that we had accepted the end of rule of law in relations with Russia. The complex European project, which the United States led for nearly 50 years would be put in question. We would be faced with a rogue power (Russia) playing as desired among several weak and insecure countries such as the Baltics, Georgia, or Moldova. America's own security would be threatened. The freedom of movement of our diplomacy would be severely limited by the instability throughout the region.

This freedom of movement will be especially important to protect in the new international conditions which are emerging in the 21st century. Coming years will be characterized by the emergence of new powers, by new and untested crisis situations and by the rapid spread of high-speed information technology. Maintaining a coherent foreign policy will become many times more difficult. The United States will succeed only if it is able to build a sense of cohesion among new powers and old. To do this, we must maintain the leading role of Western values and methods in the new information networks. Losing the advantage to Russia would undercut this interest severely. We would find ourselves on the defensive. We would be unable to take initiatives to maintain our technological advantage. This is one reason why Russia is spending so much on propaganda and information technology. It wants to steal the narrative and has succeeded already to a considerable extent.

*Question.* Is Germany a mediator in the Ukraine conflict or a genuine supporter of Ukraine's desire to join Europe?

Answer. Germany rejects the idea that it is mediating in this crisis. Chancellor Merkel has taken the lead, because she has the best contacts with Putin and because Germany has serious interests in Russia. But as her quick trip to Washington in February demonstrated, Chancellor Merkel conducts her diplomacy with the closest consultation with the United States and the European allies. From the first days of post-Soviet Ukrainian independence, Germany has been among the strongest supporters of Ukraine's sovereignty and economic stability. It supported Ukraine's desire to move closer to Europe, because it believed this was the best way to ensure both the security and economic independence of Ukraine.

*Question.* Can U.S. leadership in Ukraine be supplanted by German leadership? If so, is this desirable or conducive to the advancement of American national interests?

Answer. No, Germany cannot take over leadership from the United States in Ukraine or elsewhere in Europe. The Germans are the first to state that without American support, there could be no European defense or diplomacy with Russia. As I mentioned during my testimony, I believe that the United States has put too much burden on Germany during this crisis. Chancellor Merkel is a brilliant, dedicated leader, but neither she nor her country have the background or the resources to be the major Russian interlocutor with the West. Germany would be in a better position if there were a more active American role. Not taking over the negotiations, but participating in both words and deeds. It is at this moment not clear whether Putin believes he can push through his goals with the Europeans, while the United States stands by. Testing his intentions is too big a risk to take. it is important that he be clear that the United States will react if he pushes further forward than he already has.

---

RESPONSE OF JOHN HERBST TO QUESTION
SUBMITTED BY SENATOR BOB CORKER

*Question.* Given the magnitude of the threat and challenges posed by Russian aggression in Ukraine, has the United States devoted sufficient attention and resources to this issue? What more can and should be done?

Answer. A revisionist Kremlin bent on overturning the post-cold-war settlement in Eurasia is the greatest threat to global stability and American interests at this

68

moment. The American response to this suggests that the White House does not understand this danger. That response has been reactive, piecemeal and, overall, ineffective.

This danger is currently manifest in Ukraine. What we face today is not a Ukraine crisis, but a crisis of Kremlin aggression which appeared earlier in Georgia and today in Ukraine. To address this challenge, we need a comprehensive policy with at least six elements.

First we need to accurately and publicly define the challenge. Nowhere has the White House laid out the challenge to Eurasian and global stability posed by Mr. Putin's revanchist policies.

If the administration correctly defines the problem, it will be clear that the United States must take the lead in resolving it—the second element of a sound policy. We cannot subcontract leadership on this issue to Berlin or any other capital because our vital interests are involved. So, for instance we would insist that the United States must be part of the negotiating process that produced the cease-fires.

We would also develop strong and proactive policies imposing major costs on the Kremlin for its aggression. This leads us to the third and fourth elements of our policy.

The third is to impose economic costs on Moscow for its aggression by economic sanctions. Washington has done a pretty good job on this front in pulling an, at times, reluctant Europe to levy sanctions.

But the fourth element relates to the military. Ukrainian forces have done a commendable job fighting the strongest military in Europe. We should openly and unapologetically be providing Ukraine substantial military equipment, including defensive lethal weapons, to deter further Russian aggression in Ukraine or, if deterrence fails, to impose a higher cost on Russian forces. This cost might help ultimately stop Kremlin aggression in Ukraine; but even if it does not achieve that, it will leave Moscow with fewer military resources to carry out aggression elsewhere. At a minimum, our policy should be designed to make the war in Ukraine so unpleasant for Moscow that it decides it is too expensive to unleash war beyond that country.

Fifth, we need to exert our leadership in NATO and push for the deployment of far more substantial forces and equipment to the Baltic countries and perhaps other eastern members of the alliance. The purpose is to deter possible Kremlin provocations there.

Finally, we need to provide even more additional resources to Radio Free Europe and Radio Libert to increase its Russian language programming to help offset the massive Kremlin propaganda program.

These six elements will secure our vital interests against the rogue policies of Mr. Putin.

One last point. The administration is not devoting sufficient intelligence resources to the Russian war in Ukraine and the broader Kremlin danger. This flows naturally, but unfortunately, from the failure to understand the gravity of the danger. This needs to change.

———

RESPONSE OF VICTORIA NULAND TO QUESTION
SUBMITTED BY SENATOR JAMES E. RISCH

*Question.* A few months after the Russian invasion of Georgia, President Obama was unwilling to provide defensive military equipment to the Georgian Government; this opposition also led to European allies refusing to provide any level of military equipment to Georgia. While President Obama has refused to provide defensive lethal arms to Ukraine, does the U.S. position support other nations offering military assistance to Ukraine, or will the administration seek to block those provisions as well?

Answer. The administration has not taken a position on other nations providing security assistance to Ukraine. In fact, we have worked closely with a number of allies and partners to encourage them to contribute greater security assistance to Ukraine. Solidarity among allies is essential to our response to Russian aggression. Russia's aggression in Ukraine makes clear that European security and the international rules and norms against territorial aggression cannot be taken for granted. Together with Europe, we are supporting the Ukrainian people as they choose their own future and develop their democracy and economy.

While we continue to believe that there is no military resolution to this crisis, Ukraine has the right to defend itself. We have committed significant nonlethal security assistance to help Ukraine sustain its defense and internal security operations.

The interagency is conducting an ongoing review of our elements of security assistance to Ukraine to ensure they are responsive, appropriate, and calibrated to achieve our objectives. We continue to monitor the situation closely and remain in constant contact with our Ukrainian counterparts, as well as our NATO allies and partners, to explore opportunities for defense cooperation.

———

RESPONSES OF BRIAN P. MCKEON TO QUESTIONS
SUBMITTED BY SENATOR JAMES E. RISCH

EUROPEAN REASSURANCE INITIATIVE

*Question.* In your testimony you mentioned the European Reassurance Initiative and the success of the ERI among our eastern European allies. Unfortunately, ERI was not placed in the Defense Department's base budget; and as a result has created some concern among European allies about an enduring U.S. commitment to the initiative.

♦ Will you ensure the ERI is included in the base FY17 budget?

Answer. The European Reassurance Initiative (ERI) is an important tool for U.S. efforts to reassure our allies and partners, and it is critical that these efforts continue for as long as necessary. The Department's FY 2016 Overseas Contingency Operations (OCO) request includes $789.3 million in ERI funding to sustain the efforts started in FY 2015 and reflects our continued commitment to the initiative. The source of the funds will be considered against competing global priorities, legal requirements, and the constraints imposed by the Budget Control Act before a final decision is made for the FY 2017 budget.

*Question.* In your testimony you mentioned the European Reassurance Initiative and the success of the ERI among our eastern European allies. Unfortunately, ERI was not placed in the Defense Department's base budget; and as a result has created some concern among European allies about an enduring U.S. commitment to the initiative.

♦ What additional steps can the United States take to increase the level reassurance?

Answer. The United States is committed to the security of our Central and Eastern European allies in promoting regional security. We will continue our reassurance measures through a persistent presence of air, land, and sea forces in the region. The Department's request of $789.3 million for the European Reassurance Initiative (ERI) fiscal year 2016 reflects this commitment. Additionally, we plan to increase the capability, readiness, and responsiveness of allies and partners by continuing to increase the number of exercises and training events, improve infrastructure, build partner capacity, and enhance prepositioned U.S. equipment in the region. In support of NATO's Readiness Action Plan (RAP), the United States will also participate in NATO's new Very High Readiness Joint Task Force (VJTF); increase the number of servicemembers we have assigned to Multinational Corps Northeast in Poland; and assign staff officers to the six new NATO Force Integration Units that NATO Defense Ministers agreed to establish at their February 2015 meeting.

Through both a fully funded FY 2016 ERI appropriation and the U.S. commitment to NATO's RAP/VJTF, our Eastern European allies will see results regardless of whether funding is appropriated in the base budget or the Overseas Contingency Operations (OCO) budget.

www.ingramcontent.com/pod-product-compliance
Lightning Source LLC
Chambersburg PA
CBHW081240280526
45787CB00006B/2739